A HANDS-ON GUIDE TO PERSONAL BIBLE STUDY

GETTING
THE MESSAGE

Gilbert Lennox
with foreword by Stuart Briscoe

CEDAR HILL TRUST
CONTEMPORARY CHRISTIAN COMMUNICATION

5 Cedar Hill, Ballycraigy Road
Newtownabbey, Co Antrim, N Ireland

Getting the Message
Copyright © 2003 by Gilbert Lennox
Published by Cedar Hill Trust
ISBN 0-9546694-0-1

Printed in Northern Ireland

For
Heather
Kristyn
Jenni
Michael
Simon

CONTENTS

FOREWORD

For many centuries the Bible has been the world's best selling book. But while it still sells briskly it must be admitted that it is probably the world's least read best seller. And there are understandable reasons for this. People still tend to revere this ancient book, sometimes treating it as some kind of sacred icon. You've heard them say, "I swear on the Bible" when they are either strenuously denying something or trying in vain to convince someone. Revere it they might but read it they don't.

More often than not they have been led to believe that it is either irrelevant or too difficult to understand. Irrelevant because it was written so long ago that the modern world has moved on past it, difficult because its ideas are so different from modern ideas and its language far removed from contemporary ways of communicating.

Gilbert Lennox is well aware of these issues and has taken the time to write *Getting the Message* first of all to encourage people to see the value and relevance of the Bible, and secondly to show them how to go about reading it with understanding.

Notice that I didn't say he tells you how to do it. Because he doesn't. He shows you how to do it with practical step by step models and examples.

This is a most helpful and needed book and I warmly commend Gilbert for writing it. I trust you will be enriched by delving into it, getting the message and putting its message into practice.

Stuart Briscoe, November 2003

ACKNOWLEDGMENTS

A teenage incident is indelibly imprinted on my mind. Saturday afternoon; I rush into the house from football practice to discover my mum sitting down from meal preparation to read the Psalms. Not wanting to disturb her, I open the lounge door to discover my dad, snatching a brief hour from work, on his knees in the front room, his Bible open on the chair before him.

This was not a film set. Nor was it an isolated occurrence. Whatever else I might have thought of my parents through teenage eyes, however culturally outdated and irrelevant their church life might have been to my generation, their faith was not an act, nor even a habit: it was lived. Central to it was their encounter with God through his Word. I am so grateful for this legacy.

I am grateful also to those who took time to help me walk for myself through Scripture. To DWG especially for the long and patient hours spent teaching me how to think biblically and opening my spiritual imagination; to many different groups of students who allowed me to practise on them what I was learning, to JCL for his example and encouragement, and to the good folks at Glenabbey for being the best possible environment in which to learn and teach the Word during the past 16 years.

Two groups of people deserve particular thanks: Noel R, Stephen S, Clifford T, and Robert Y, who have prodded me gently but effectively to finish this guide, supporting, shaping and believing all the way through; and the production team: Michael H for his hours of enthusiastic work in the design and preparation of the artwork, Linda M. for her attention to detail, and David Y. for his illustrations. I am also grateful to Stuart, not just for the foreword, but for his advice and encouragement at crucial moments during my life.

And then my family – that amazing bunch who fill our home and life with such love, energy, fun and potential. To my wife, for commitment bordering on the miraculous, the greatest debt of thanks is owed. And thanks, kids, for putting up with my poor attempts at humour and late night writing absences. If for no one else, I have written this for you.

FIRST WORDS

If you have never before engaged in the process of personal study of the Bible you are about to embark on a very special adventure. In some senses I envy you the beginning!

I am so grateful for a conversation I had over thirty years ago that was to change and shape the rest of my life. Conversation is perhaps not the right word. He talked, I listened. I needed to. With superb timing, this man who had known me since childhood challenged my ill-disciplined mind with his passion for Scripture, pouring health-giving words into me, mostly – I found out later – from Paul's advice and strong pleading with his young friend Timothy. He even bought me my lunch so that he could continue the conversation!

The passion rubbed off. It launched me into an often wrong-headed and stumbling, but ultimately fantastically rewarding journey which still has me in its grip, still shocks and exhilarates, confounds and challenges. It is this journey that I want to share.

The Bible is unlike any other book in history. Not merely in its composition – written by over 40 different authors, in different countries, using different languages and over a period of some 1600 years. Nor even in its popularity as the world's runaway best seller, nor even in its unparalleled influence throughout thousands of years of history. **It is unique in its source.** It is God's Word written. It is truth. The words, as Jesus taught his followers, are "spirit and they are life."[1] This is no mere handbook to life: this is God revealing himself personally to us.

[1] John 6:63

This sets it apart from any other work of literature. And it means that the approach we take to our study of it is not that of a critic, but, if we have come to faith in the divine author, of a worshipper. We do not come to the Bible as consumers but as servants. We do not sit in judgement upon its truth; we seek to allow its truth to sit in judgement upon us.

Jesus taught that his words provide us the only sufficient basis on which to build our entire life, confident that when the storms rage, the foundation will not give way.[2] We might not always see the connection between a regular hour or two of thoughtful and prayerful Bible reading every week and 'real life'. But there will come times when something malfunctions, when the comfortable script we have been writing for ourselves is torn up by the unforeseen. It is then that our understanding of God, his ways, his wisdom and his love that we have cultivated over the years through interaction with his Word will provide the solid core we need for faith and for survival.

[2] Matthew 7:24-27

Airline pilots receive rigorous and regular training, right up to the end of their career. The fact that no other profession involves the charge of 300 people travelling at 33,000 feet at speeds of over 600 mph may have something to do with this! Each pilot hopes that the unthinkable will never happen. The reality is, however, that for some all the years of training, all the patient hours of disciplined work on the simulator, all of the experience of flying could be tested without notice in a matter of a few seconds, with the lives of hundreds of people dependent upon the outcome.

What if something similar were to happen to you? What if the whole issue of your life, the life of your family or of your church were to hinge on such a test? How would you do if, like Joseph, you were suddenly called to appear before the world's super power with the opportunity to witness to the reality of the Living God? How would you do if, again like Joseph, you had the boss's spouse offering sexual favours to you every single day? Have you built into your life sufficient disciplined personal encounter with God through his Word that you know God's way, and are utterly convinced his way is right, to the point where you will remain loyal to him, whatever the personal cost?

The stakes are high, much higher than many of us imagine.

God's word is as priceless treasure: it does not lie on the earth's surface waiting to be picked up by the casual day-tripper or tourist, but has to be dug for, to be discovered and mined. God's word is as gourmet food: it doesn't come shrink wrapped and pre-cooked, it cannot be micro-waved, but requires patient and careful preparation. There is no quick fix.

Instead, there is the patient, gracious Holy Spirit, ready to reward those who diligently seek, who weave the Word into the fabric of every day, who understand that to be a disciple is to be a learner, is to submit to the authority of Jesus Christ – an authority which comes to us through his words.

No fruit is produced without endurance. What springs up quickly, withers as quickly. Roots, if they are to hold, need to go down deep.

It is my prayer that you will make the thoughtful reading of God's Word a habit that shapes character and life and that in increasing measure you experience an on-going encounter with the living, majestic Lord Jesus through his Word.

To encourage you in this I will borrow some words from an author who had an important influence on me in my late teens. While I echo his experience, I'm really only beginning myself.

Bible study has torn apart my life and remade it. That is to say that God, through his Word, has done so. In the darkest periods of my life when everything seemed hopeless, I would struggle in the grey dawns of many faraway countries to grasp the basic truths of Scripture passages. I looked for no immediate answers to my problems. Only did I sense intuitively that I was drinking drafts from a fountain that gave life to my soul.
Slowly as I grappled with textual and theological problems, a strength grew deep within me. Foundations cemented themselves to an other-worldly rock beyond the reach of time and space, and I became strong and more alive. If I could write poetry about it I would. If I could sing through paper, I would

flood your soul with the glorious melodies that express what I have found. I cannot exaggerate for there are no expressions majestic enough to tell of the glory I have seen or of the wonder of finding that I, a neurotic, unstable, middle-aged man have my feet firmly planted in eternity and breathe the air of heaven. And all this has come to me through a careful study of Scripture. [3]

[3] John White, The Fight, Inter-Varsity Press, 1977, pp 54–55

GETTING STARTED

Carol had recently become a Christian. She had been going along to the student group with Lisa since freshers' week, attracted initially by the warmth and reality of friendship, and then increasingly by the message about Jesus. She had started to read a copy of John's Gospel and after three months had become deeply convinced of her need to commit her life to Christ. Lisa bought her a New Testament and avidly she began to read. At least at the start. She quickly discovered that there was more to it than she had imagined. She began to feel frustrated, sensing there was so much more to it than she was seeing, finding some things hard to grasp. She wasn't sure how to proceed and no one seemed able to help her...

John had been a Christian since he was a child, brought up in an evangelical background with Bibles everywhere. His knowledge of Scripture seemed to have infiltrated his life without much conscious effort on his part. In fact he couldn't remember ever having read a book of the Bible at a sitting. He could quote verses, knew all kinds of facts, knew what he believed and sometimes even why. But somehow the Bible wasn't a living book to him. He wished it were. But time demands, work, family soon frustrated his annual attempts to get into the Bible for himself...

Sarah led the small group. She was good with people and had been a Christian for four years now. They were studying Romans, and the study guide had some very helpful questions, which provoked discussion. But as she reflected on things after five weeks, she wondered if anyone really had learned anything. She couldn't remember very much from the first few studies, and had an uneasy feeling that their times together were more 'share your ignorance sessions' than anything else...

The reality of many people's uneasy relationship with the Bible forced itself onto my agenda during a student weekend retreat. In an impromptu survey among the 70 or so students present I discovered that the average amount of time spent per day by each student in some contact with the Bible was five minutes. Some of these Christian students admitted to spending no time at all. Yet all had invested in attending a Bible teaching weekend.

This contradiction between desire and reality in the area of personal Bible study seems to be repeated in the lives of most followers of Christ some of the time, and in the lives of many most of the time.

CORE FACTORS IN OUR STRUGGLE

There are a number of factors involved in the struggles that many have with personal Bible reading and study. To be sure, some believers are apathetic in their spiritual lives, and for them the term 'struggle' is not really appropriate – they have given up any struggle there was long ago. It is very unlikely that you fall into that category, however, for unless you had a desire to deepen your encounter with God's Word you would not have picked up this guide. Many, like you, are looking for an increasing spiritual reality in life and suspect (rightly) that spending time in Scripture might well have something to do with it, yet feel powerless to do anything about it.

I DON'T KNOW HOW

The first major factor that has emerged time and time again in discussions is that many simply do not know how to go about their personal study of the Word of God.

Even those with a good level of formal education often seem to find it hard to apply the skills they have learned to their study of Scripture. The resulting frustration is only compounded by guilt each time some well-intentioned speaker focuses on the importance of personal Bible study. The cycle of exhortation-guilt-attempt-failure-frustration is hard to overcome.

As followers of Jesus Christ, we should need no convincing that it is important to spend time in his Word. (However, we do need reminding from time to time!) But where do we start? How do we go about it? How can we be sure that our interpretation is right, or does that not really matter? How do we know what is the voice of God and what is the product of an overheated imagination? We need to be shown a realistic way of setting about our study so that we can experience at least some success to motivate us to keep going. That is the purpose of this guide.

There are many books on the topic of personal Bible study, and at the end of this guide I have provided a list of those that I have found especially helpful. This guide has a particular focus: **its purpose is to take you through the process of personal Bible study through the study of two short biblical books.**

Now some may be somewhat wary here. "Not another method!" might be the reaction, especially if you have already tried (and struggled with) other methods. At the same time a method may be exactly what others are looking for.

If we understand method as a helpful yet flexible way of organising our approach to Bible study, then, yes, I will be sharing a method. But I have no interest in championing the 'Gilbert Lennox Way', as opposed to some other method. My concern is to help you find a way to successful personal Bible study as a practical reality in your life.

My 'method', such as it is, at its heart consists of learning to ask key questions that can help to unlock the Bible for us. Some of these questions you will find helpful, some may not be so helpful. That's fine by me. There is no rigid system here, no complicated rules that must be followed in exactly the right order or we fail the test! Think of it more in terms of practical guidance, suggestions, personal coaching as you set about your own study. For it is important that you believe that **YOU CAN DO THIS!** You don't need an advanced degree in hermeneutics (the science and art of interpretation) or biblical languages.

Learn what you can from this guide, and discard the rest. Combine some of the ideas here with ideas you have picked up elsewhere. Use charts or don't use them. Use colour coding or don't use it. Draw diagrams or don't draw diagrams. What matters is not the particular method – it is the reality of encountering God through the thoughtful and careful reading of his Word.

I MEAN WELL, BUT...

The second major factor in folk's struggles with personal Bible study is personal discipline: few of us are consistently disciplined self-starters. On our own we can so easily lose our way, run out of steam and become discouraged. Most of us therefore benefit greatly when we have others to walk with us, to learn beside us, to encourage us along.

I have sought to design this guide to act as a companion through the process. But of course it is rather unresponsive! This is why a central suggestion of this guide is that you **seek out someone to study along with you.** If keeping on with your good intentions has been a problem for you, why not, at this early stage, identify someone who will agree to walk through this process with you?

Whatever it takes! The fact is that this guide is guaranteed to be utterly useless to you... **UNLESS** you commit yourself to the process it outlines.

Reading through the details of a revolutionary new fitness programme might fire your imagination and even make you feel fitter. But there is no virtual reality way to physical fitness. Bible study is like that. You actually have to DO something.

I HAVEN'T TIME

The third major factor (often the first in our own minds) is time. There seems to be so little of it to go around. Life in the Western world has gathered pace in the past 25 years or so. All the time- and labour-saving devices have left us neither less tired nor with more time. We seem to have to run harder to stand still.

We need to remind ourselves on occasions of two things:

- First, we have exactly the same amount of time as everyone else: 7 days per week, 24 hours per day, 60 minutes per hour.
- Second, we have all the time there is.

If we are to **find time** with God's Word we are going to have to **make time.** It is a matter of priority, of values. It may also be a matter of better personal management. The fact is that we tend to find time for those things that we really value – as opposed to those things we say that we value. Something of lesser value may have to go.

Allied to this is the importance of understanding and respecting how we best function. I remember reading the lives of some of the great spiritual giants of the past. I was struck by how early they tended to rise in the morning for prayer and Bible reading. I tried it and nearly collapsed under the stress. Only then did I discover that they went to bed about four hours earlier than I did. The rhythm of life changes from culture to culture, and even to some degree from person to person. Some of us are early morning people, some late night people. The rhythm varies also with age, family and work requirements. We need to find a time when we are alert, fully functional and can make a protected time space for ourselves.

It seems where I live that almost everyone is always tired! Given the pace and demands of modern living, some tiredness is inevitable, some is even healthy! But some is a result of poor choices, poor lifestyle, lack of discipline.

And some is even purely psychological. The desire for rest, for comfort, for undemanding entertainment overcomes many of us in the twilight zone despite the good intentions of the early part of the day. It is so much easier towards the end of a long day to switch on the television (and switch off our minds) than it is to take out our Bible, not to mention a notebook.

An old sage once taught his students: "say 'no' to something every day, just to keep in the habit!" However, contemporary Western culture appears to be based increasingly on the individual's right first to define what happiness is, and then to seek it at all costs. Saying 'no' is not easy – but it is remarkable once we actually get started, against our feelings, to some thoughtful Bible reading, that time often slips by unnoticed.

The tough truth is that if we are going to make time for Bible study it will take more than the belief that such study is worthwhile and it will take more than a genuine desire to do it. It will take personal discipline and good planning, not just a new year's resolution. I constantly meet people who have started the year with yet another resolution to make it through the Bible, only to founder after the Flood! Genesis 1-11 must be the most read chapters in the Bible. Despite our good intentions, somehow we soon find ourselves submerged in the reality of daily survival and the Bible increasingly gets pushed to one side.

Now most of us react to discipline in our 'free time' the way my kids react to the mention of housework! The temptation is to lie down until the idea goes away. Courage! No pain, no gain! We need to break through this psychological sound barrier and get started.

So let's be practical: **when are YOU going to make the time?**

BE REALISTIC

Why not be realistic and begin with **one hour per week** - one protected hour – at a time when you are more or less functional! Select one morning, or evening, or other time each week when you can set aside an hour for personal study, in addition to the time you spend daily reading Scripture and reading devotional notes. Who knows, over time one hour may change into two without you really noticing it, because the discipline develops into something closer to delight and you discover that the rewards more than justify the effort.

I could, of course, emphasise the point by expressing one hour in terms of being less than 1% of the average waking week; or as just over half the length of the average film; as equivalent to three coffee breaks; or as a quarter of a night out with your friends. But I won't.

WHERE SHOULD I START?

Where to begin? It is here that indecision plagues so many people. Imagine a child being sent out to buy a loaf of bread and being faced with a choice of 66 varieties, none of which she has have ever seen before. They are all so different in size, in texture, in taste – she might be so overwhelmed that she ends up leaving the shop without buying anything. It can be like that when it comes to the Bible, especially if we are new to it.

We need to start somewhere. In fact, since I'm Irish, I am going to suggest that we start in two places at once! In other words that we have two parallel approaches: in the one we focus on the unity of the Bible by following the story line through and building our active knowledge of its entire library. In the other we focus on the diversity of the Bible, and take its books one at a time for more in-depth reading.

UNITY IN DIVERSITY

The folks who start in Genesis 1 are on to a good thing – **if they keep going** beyond the flood - for reading through the Bible from start to finish is perhaps the best way to grasp the fundamental unity of the big picture.

The Bible is not simply an anthology or collection of individual books. Within the diversity of individual titles there is a **central narrative unity**: that is, the Bible is basically **telling one story.** Every individual book contributes in a unique way to the plot, the core story line as it moves from creation to new creation.

This story line can be set out as follows:

- Creation: the origin, nature and purpose of human life within the universe
- The Fall and the promise of a divine solution through a coming One
- Preparation for the coming of Messiah through the emergence and training of the Hebrew nation (Genesis to Malachi)
- The coming of Messiah, his life, death and resurrection (The Gospels)
- The age of the Church (Acts and the New Testament letters)

- The consummation of history (Revelation – although it has a much broader scope than this)

It is so important, especially if we are new to the Bible, that we read this story, and build up for ourselves an understanding of how the Bible fits together. In this way we can read the significance of the individual parts against the whole. (You will find more detail concerning the movements in Old Testament history in Chapter 13.)

As we do this we will notice the striking **thematic unity.** This unity is to be expected since it is God's revelation of himself to us so that we can come to know him, and reflect him in the way we order our lives. Yet it is still remarkable that when we consider such issues as the nature of God, or teaching on controversial subjects such as sexual expression or the afterlife, we find that the Bible speaks to these in a harmonious, unified way. Indeed, no one part of the Bible tells us all there is to know on any major issue, but as we piece together, for example, what Genesis, the Psalms, Hebrews and 2 Peter teach about the origin of the universe, we find a single voice emerging, a clear point of view.

As a result it has been possible for students of the Bible to distil its core teachings under individual headings such as 'the Church', 'salvation', 'the ministry of the Holy Spirit'. It follows that it is very important for us not to rest our entire understanding of a particular issue in Scripture solely on one verse, or even one section of the Bible, unless the issue is not dealt with anywhere else.

From the unity of the Bible we draw the conclusion that our first major approach to Bible study must be to **consider it as a whole.**

DIVERSITY IN UNITY

At the same time, within the unity of the Bible there is enormous diversity. God has chosen to reveal himself in a library of **individual books** which were not all written down at one time, in one culture, in one language by one person. Rather it was written over a period of around 1600 years, in different languages, cultures, and geographical settings by a wide variety of people from different walks of life.

The word 'bible' itself highlights this, for it means 'little books'. God could, of course, have revealed himself differently, for example through a series of wise sayings or philosophical statements; or even by means of a neatly packaged and organised theological system, properly indexed so that we could look up any topic and check out what God says about it. Instead of this he has given us a fascinating variety of individual books, each different from the rest, spanning a variety of genre such as sweeping historical accounts, poetry, letters, wisdom literature and prophecy, to name a few.

In the understanding that God is by definition the supreme teacher in the universe, this is surely more than a hint that he means us to read his revelation the way he chose to express it – that is by considering the Bible, **one book at a time.**

This should not replace our general reading of the whole Bible, otherwise we will not be able to see the individual book as part of a bigger picture. But if we are going to grasp the whole, then we need to grow in our understanding of the individual parts, so that we grasp what is the unique and vital message of Genesis, or Romans or Haggai.

From the diversity of the Bible we draw the conclusion that the second major approach to Bible study is to engage in the study of individual books. This is what will occupy most space in this guide.

FOCUS ON ONE BOOK

In the early days of my relationship with the Bible I was totally daunted by the amount of material it contained, and as a result kept dipping into different parts of the Bible in a desperate attempt to grasp as much as possible as quickly as possible. While this did some good, it left me thoroughly dissatisfied and frustrated. So I was ready for the wise advice that came my way: settle for a while on one book, get to know it thoroughly - "until your finger prints are all over it" was the exact expression! It turned out to be one of the most rewarding experiences, and has shaped and formed my life and service ever since.

WHICH BOOK?

But which book should we choose?

More choices! And if we are not careful we can end up like rabbits caught in the headlights of our own indecision.

It's actually not as simple a question as it may first appear, for the Bible is not only a library of books, it is a library of **different kinds** of books. It contains letters and gospels, poetry, stories, great historical sagas, books of law and prophecy.

One of the central principles in Bible study is that we need to learn to approach each different genre of biblical literature in a way appropriate to it. Poetry needs to be approached as poetry, gospels as gospels, prophecy as prophecy and so on. So, which book do we choose?

It may be some time since you read a novel, read a work of history or studied a legal document. It may be even longer since you read any poetry. The chances are, however, that you have read and still read letters – and even write one or two, or at least an occasional e-mail. **The letters of the New Testament make a good place to start,** especially the shorter ones, as we are familiar with the basic format, even though one or two of the letter writing conventions of the first century are no longer in common use.

In addition, the New Testament letters contain the teaching given by God through his apostles and prophets to the early church. As such, of course, they have a very immediate appeal and application to us since we are part of that same movement in history. You may find the letters more accessible than other books, especially if you are more or less a beginner to serious Bible study.

Which letter? Here I suggest that we **start with a book that can be read at a sitting,** so that we can grasp its overall content without enormous effort. Romans has 16 chapters, Titus has 3. You could read Titus perhaps five times in an hour, Romans once. So choose a short book to begin with, one that you can read several times at a sitting.

For the purposes of this guide, therefore, I have chosen a short letter: Paul's letter to the **Philippians.** For the moment the most important thing is that we start somewhere.

This means that the study approach suggested in the first part of this guide is tailored to reading and studying the letters of the New Testament. This is necessary, and one of the reasons why more rigid methods of Bible study can come unstuck. The poetry of the Psalms should not be approached in the same way as the prose of the letters.

At the same time, many of the questions and principles of study which we will develop in the context of the New Testament letters will also apply to the study of other biblical books. Certain questions are always helpful, certain principles are always necessary when it comes to Bible study, no matter what book is being studied.

In addition, in the final units of this guide we will look specifically at other types of biblical literature, especially in the Old Testament, and suggest both some modifications to our general approach, and some new tools that we will need to add to our kit. And we will have the opportunity to try these out on the Book of Ruth.

In a moment I'm going to ask you to stop, get something to write with and something to write on – pencil and notebook, computer, whatever - grab a cup of coffee or equivalent and come back here ready to begin. But there is a final question we must consider.

WHICH VERSION OF THE BIBLE SHOULD WE USE?

Unless you read the original languages of the Bible – Hebrew (most of the Old Testament), Aramaic (a sister language to Hebrew, used in two passages in Ezra and half of Daniel), and New Testament Greek (not the same as modern Greek) – you are reading a translation. It is obviously to our advantage if in our study we use the best translation available to us.

The history of Bible translation is a fascinating and inspiring story. For many years the Latin Vulgate translation of Jerome (AD 400) was the standard. The fact that it was hand copied (the printing press had not yet been invented) and the fact that literacy was not as widespread as it is today meant that even in translation the Bible was accessible to very few.

The first complete English translation of the Bible was the work of John Wycliff, although it was only a translation from the Latin Vulgate and contained many inaccuracies. Oxford scholar William Tyndale, deeply challenged by the ignorance of the Bible among even the clergy, dedicated himself to the task of translating the Bible from the original languages into English. In order to achieve this goal he had to leave England, such was the official opposition. His translation of the New Testament was printed at Worms in 1525, and had to be smuggled into Britain. Tyndale himself was strangled and then burned for his efforts, before he could complete the Old Testament. Nevertheless, his translation had great influence, and approximately 90% of his words found their way into the King James Version (1611).

Despite the opposition, the desire to have the Bible in one's own language and based on the translation of the original documents became unstoppable, and not just in the English-speaking world.[4]

[4] For example in Germany where Luther's translation, completed by 1532, became the official German translation.

The translation by a committee of scholars, sponsored by King James I (the King James Version or Authorised Version) published in 1611, was a landmark event for English speakers and has exerted enormous and well-deserved influence. This was followed in English by a Revised Version (1881) which preserved the language of the KJV, but which took into account more recent discoveries in biblical manuscripts, and is therefore more accurate (although more difficult to read).

WHY ALL THE DIFFERENT TRANSLATIONS?

Translation of the Bible in English did not stop there, however, for three major reasons.

First, **the way we use language changes** over time. This happens for a variety of reasons – for example, international influence or new developments in science and technology. The result is that many of the words or phrases that communicated clearly in the 17th (or even the 19th) Century, have either changed meaning or fallen into disuse, and as a result can easily cause confusion if used today. In the desire to ensure that the unchanging Word communicates readily with changing cultures, various bodies have undertaken either partial revisions, or brand new translations.[5]

Second, **developments in the science of textual criticism.** By this I mean the process by which translators arrive at the most accurate source text for their translations. This is vitally important work since before we translate we need to know, for example, if what we are translating is what Paul, or David actually wrote. Since none of the original manuscripts of the books of the Bible exist (that we are aware of), scholars need to apply very rigorous techniques in deciding on the text which is as close as possible to the original wording. Continual study of the extant manuscripts of the Bible, together with increasing understanding of how the original languages were used, yield new insights which can be incorporated into revisions or new translations.

Third, developing **theories of translation.** By 'theory of translation' I mean the principles upon which translators decide which words and phrases in English (or other modern language) best convey the meaning of the original. Some translators place the emphasis on 'word for word' accuracy, although in its purest form the result would be unreadable, since grammar and idiom vary greatly from language to language. Others place the emphasis on the communication of meaning through modern idiom.

As a result, the twentieth century saw a number of major new translations such as the New English Bible and the widely popular New International Version. It also saw a number of 'freer translations' such as the Good News Bible, the Living Bible and The Message. The result is that if you enter a Christian bookshop in the West you will probably be faced with a dizzying array of Bibles.

Since **the basic tool of Bible study must be a good translation,** which should we choose?

I suggest that where you have a choice – and remember that many millions of believers throughout the world do not – you should choose a version of the Bible:

[5] For someone new to this discussion it is important to stress that no other ancient document is so well attested. The number of surviving ancient manuscripts of all or part of the New Testament is unprecedented – over 5,000. While there are around 150,000 variant readings, almost all have to do with changes in spelling, grammatical mistakes which are obvious, and accidental omissions or repetitions of words. Less than 2% of the text is in any doubt, and none of these doubts affects in any way either the major events or the major teachings.

- based on the best original manuscripts
- known for its faithfulness to the original text
- and which reads well to modern ears

The trouble is that it is probably impossible to find one version that successfully combines literal translation with the more dynamic translation required to communicate well to modern minds. My suggestion is that you use at least **two versions** rather than one.

For example, as my main study Bible I use the New International Version (NIV) which in addition to being one of the more accurate translations has the advantage of very wide acceptance and it reads quite well. As a constant reference, however, I use the New American Standard Bible (NASB) which is more of a 'word for word' translation (and reads rather woodenly as a result, although it has more recently been helpfully revised).

For those who would like a more in-depth treatment of this issue, I recommend the helpful discussion by Gordon Fee and Douglas Stuart.[6] However – and this may stir your blood - I would strongly recommend that when it comes to your actual study of the Bible you avoid the King James Version, and that you avoid freer translations such as the Living Bible or The Message. General reading is a different matter. Particularly in the Old Testament, some of the poetic expression of the King James is unsurpassed. In addition, more modern versions such as the New Living Translation make reading through some of the longer books of the Old Testament a much more gripping experience than would be the case with, for example, the New American Standard Bible. If you have access to a variety of versions by all means read them all! Gordon Fee recommends that before we study a particular passage we should read it in at least seven versions.[7]

In addition to the number of versions of the Bible, there is increasing variety in the way these versions are packaged and presented. You can purchase, a 'Woman's Devotional Bible', a 'Spirit-filled Life Bible', a 'Prophecy Bible'. While all of these answer particular interests and needs, in the end they might prove to be more of a distraction from the kind of personal study this guide seeks to foster.[8] (I shall be referring to the use of commentaries and other helps at a later stage.)

But now it's time to pause for refreshment, get your notebook, and return ready to begin!

[6] Gordon Fee and Douglas Stuart, How to read the Bible for all its worth, Scripture Union, 1994, pp 28-44

[7] Gordon Fee, New Testament Exegesis, Westminster John Knox Press, 2002, p 11

[8] An exception to this would be the NIV study Bible which many have found to be an excellent basic tool with its maps, mini-concordance, introductions to each book and often helpful background information and commentary.

A REAL PAGE TURNER

Let's think for a moment of how we approach reading a letter, and in particular a letter from someone we love, rather than from the bank manager (unless, of course, they happen to be the same person!).

Snug in your favourite chair, surrounded by all kinds of reference and study materials - dictionary, atlas, thesaurus, and of course the Greek/Latin lexicon- you rip open the first page and begin: "My darling"! No longer able to restrain yourself you grab the English Grammar from the shelves and, after fifteen minutes' research, discover that, yes, 'my' is a possessive adjective. Wow! How cool is that? 'Darling' is more tricky. What precisely does it mean? You must be careful not to read too much into it, so a search around its Old English roots might be revealing. Is it merely a social convention? The Guide to Correct Usage in Letter Writing proves its worth. Your hour is up; you fold the letter and turn to other urgent business...

That is precisely the impression many have of what Bible study means. Even the word **study** fills some with dread. So relax. Please. It doesn't have to be like that. At least...

Every caricature is an exaggeration to make a point. Of course it can be helpful to have a dictionary, an atlas, a commentary, a book of background information - eventually. But don't start there. Start as you would with a letter. **Read it.**

This is the most fundamental point, yet often the most ignored. We need to read the text as it was intended to be read.

Can you imagine, when this letter arrived at Philippi, what folks in the church would have thought if someone announced that they had received a letter from Paul, proceeded to read the first eleven sentences, and then said that the rest would keep until the following week?

No one would dream of approaching a love letter like that, let alone any other piece of writing, such as a novel or a play. Nor would you dream of starting your reading a third of the way in, any more than you would study Hamlet by opening the play at random, selecting a line or two and then trying to work out what it means. You read it, **all** of it - even several times - so that you have a grasp of the content, you know the plot, you know the context.

Read it.

Don't read commentaries, notes or other guides just yet. In my life as a teacher I have known some students, even at university, who attempted to prepare themselves for literature examinations simply by reading the appropriate Critical Guide, and not by reading the text itself! This might work in terms of enabling the student to sound knowledgeable about the text (although the pretence is usually easy to detect), and might even lead to a pass mark. But it is to miss out on the entire experience of the text itself, of the power and impact of its actual words, of the mind and heart of the author.

To do this with Scripture – to spend our time solely, or even primarily, in investigating the historical and cultural background, or in reading what others have written about the text - is to miss the whole point of Scripture: **to encounter God through his word.** You can't do this by proxy, and indeed there is no need to, for the invitation to us all in the new relationship that Jesus has opened up to us is to know the Lord. Don't simply allow others to tell you about him. Come to the Word yourself and ask him to reveal himself to you by his Spirit. Encounter him for yourself. Learn first the discipline and then the art of thoughtfully reading the text. Start at the beginning and read through to the end, then do it again, and again.

A LOVE LETTER FROM HEAVEN

I have occasionally come across those who dismiss written text as 'just words on a page'. Yet it would never dawn on any of us to think that a letter from the most special person in our life is 'just words on a page' and that to spend time reading it and rereading it is a waste of time and 'not practical'. The words on the page matter for **we know the person**; and that person created us and loves us. It is the reality of the relationship that makes the words special to us and that motivates us to read them with careful, responsive intensity. This is why during those times when I have been on my travels, letters or emails from home have been so precious. This is why the soldier on the battlefield carries a letter from his or her loved one in a breast pocket.

The Bible is **a love letter from our Creator to us personally**. There is not a sentence in it that does not emerge from his wisdom and his love. It is not simply words on a page. He knows us, loves us, and wants us to know him - wants to share his thoughts with us, to convince us of his love, to inspire us with his plans, to share the very secrets of heaven with us.

Give him the opportunity. **Read Philippians,** slowly and thoughtfully, in the expectation of encountering more than words on the page.

At the same time it IS words on a page. The words are important. On those occasions when I received such letters, how I pored over those words! Every word. I didn't need any additional motivation. Every adjective, every expression – nothing was too trivial, nothing escaped my attention. Even how she signed off. In fact, being honest, I didn't usually begin at the start, I began at the end. It was vital for me to discover how she signed off. If it was "With all my love", then I could relax and enjoy myself, indulge myself in every phrase. But a "Yours sincerely" would have meant, frankly, that the rest of the letter was not worth reading!

SO, READ IT!

I have no gimmicks to offer, no quick fixes, no shortcuts, no secrets to avoid effort. If I were standing there beside you as you read, I would reach over and close this guide at this point and invite you to read Philippians. I can't do that, so all I can do is to leave a gap to remind you.

Have you read it yet? Really? Good, you are ready for the next stage, which is, believe it or not, to **read it again**.

Why read it again? Because before we begin the study of individual verses or paragraphs in the letter we need a **solid grasp of the contents of the letter as a whole.**

The teacher who did most to introduce me to the study of Scripture, told me during our very first discussion of the topic that before beginning to study any book of the Bible I should read it through no fewer than twelve times.

TWELVE TIMES! Yes, that's what I thought. I have to confess I haven't always done it, especially when faced with a book as long as Genesis! But it made the point. And come to think of it, it was never a chore to read the love letter three or four times at least at a sitting!

So take time now to read Philippians at least once more.

HOW GOOD A READER ARE YOU?

Let's think a little more about reading. Did you encounter any or all of these problems?

- It seemed to take a long time
- I didn't get anything out of it
- It raised more questions than I have answers for
- My mind kept wandering off to other things

None of these should be a cause of major worry. But there are certain things we can do to increase our enjoyment of reading.

1. If you are not a regular reader, it may well take longer than you expect, so don't allow yourself to be discouraged by what you consider to be slow. This is not a race against the clock, or against anyone else. With practice you should increase your speed at least a little. (Indeed there are books and courses available to teach 'speed reading'.) But speed is not everything, and thoughtful reading requires time.

2. The **'I didn't get anything out of it'** reaction is more complicated. First, we probably did get something out of it: for example, a firmer grasp of the content. Our reaction may well have much more to do with **feelings** of enjoyment than with the reality of genuine benefit. Second, we live in an 'instant age' – we are not used to things taking time and some of us get very impatient! Third, in the West in particular we are quite consumerist in our approach – 'what's in it for me?' There is actually a lot in Bible reading for us, but again it often takes time. Don't give up because there appears not to be an instant pay-back.

A mistake that many make is to **rush the stages of study,** impatient to get to the application. We need to learn to take our time – it will pay rich dividends, and prevent us from making hasty and erroneous applications. Cakes don't taste too good if they are taken out of the oven half way through cooking. There is a process to be respected. And in any case instant gratification is often shallow and fleeting.

Let's remember what it is that we are seeking to do. At this point we are not looking for a personal application, a 'thought for the day', a memorable sound bite or even a sermon we can try out on our friends. Rather, we are **seeking first to get to know the text** and then to allow the text to speak for itself. We need to grasp what it is saying, be guided by its emphases and allow it to set the agenda for us.

3. A third problem that can distract folks in their reading is that we soon discover that the Bible contains unpronounceable (for us) names, geographical and historical references that we do not understand, language which is not part of our everyday world, and theological terms and issues which are beyond us. The best thing I can suggest is that you rename part of your mind **The Freezer.** And into that freezer you consign most if not all of those puzzling items. They will keep quite well there until you are ready to deal with them.

4. Fourth, and perhaps most common of all, is the problem of the wandering mind. If your mind is anything like mine it takes very little for a memory to be jogged or an association to be raised so that, before I realise what is happening I have 'read' the same paragraph several times without having absorbed it. There are certain practical things that we can do here to help us, such as using an object such as a pencil (not the business end!) or even our finger to guide our focus, or even read aloud.

In the next unit we will visit this issue of reading in more detail, but one more thing before we move on:

READ PHILIPPIANS AGAIN!

READING THAT TRANSFORMS

The conversion of Augustine of Hippo is one of the great events in the history of the spread of Christianity. His mother was a devout believer and he himself had a deep knowledge of and even attraction to the faith. But he still rebelled. Until one day he heard a voice saying, "Take up and read, take up and read" – like the voice of a child who was engaged in some kind of game. This is how he describes what happened:

> *I snatched [a copy of the epistles] up, opened it, and read in silence the chapter on which my eyes first fell: "Not in rioting and drunkenness, not in chambering and impurities, not in strife and envying; but you put on the Lord Jesus Christ, and make not provision for the flesh..." No further wished I to read, nor was there need to do so. Instantly, in truth, at the end of this sentence, as if before me a peaceful light streaming into my heart, all the dark shadows of doubt fled away.* [1]

[1] Quoted in Mel Lawrenz, The Dynamics of Spiritual Formation, Baker Books, 2000, p 57

The importance of reading God's word cannot be overstated. Yet the task of encouraging people simply to read is becoming harder in our age of image. Never were there more Bibles, and never were they less read! Increasingly in the West we are becoming used to processing fast moving images rather than taking the time and employing the concentration required to read anything other than short newspaper or magazine articles, or an occasional popular novel.

You may be an honourable exception! But in reality the last time many adults read anything substantial was when they were at school or university. You may have to fight against the tide both of your own history and of contemporary culture.

If reading is a struggle, there are a number of things that we can do to help our concentration and to help us gain more from it, and therefore grow in our enjoyment and motivation to do more.

1. Listen to it read. Many folks in Bible times were unable to read – either because they had not been taught, or because 'books' were not always easily obtained. Paul reminds his young friend Timothy to "devote yourself to the public reading of Scripture" (1 Timothy 4:13). At the end of his letter to the Thessalonians he writes, "I charge you before the Lord to have this letter read to all the brothers." (1 Thessalonians 5:27). It is possible to purchase on cassette professionally recorded readings of every book of the Bible – a worthwhile investment.

For those of us who even occasionally are called upon to read the Bible in public (small group or large congregation), we should read in such a way that indicates that this is not simply the introduction to what follows, rather it is the heart of what we are doing: it is not the introduction to the message, it IS the message. If you are a preacher – slow down! Try to make the public reading of God's Word memorable.

2. Read it aloud for yourself. (You might want to make sure you are not disturbing anyone else!) Reading aloud, slowly and deliberately, is one way I frequently use to enable me to concentrate and to 'hear' Scripture. (If you don't mind the sound of your own voice, you could even record the reading and then play it back to yourself!)

3. Copy or word-process the text. This might sound like a waste of time, but again it is something I do quite frequently as I find that in copying the text I notice things that I easily miss in my normal hasty style of reading – it slows me down and forces me to focus. This is something that Kings in Israel were told that they should do – to write out their own copy of God's Word.

> *When he takes the throne of his kingdom, he is to write for himself on a scroll a copy of this law, taken from that of the priests, who are Levites. It is to be with him, and he is to read it all the days of his life so that he may learn to revere the Lord his God and follow carefully all the words of this law and these decrees and not consider himself better than his brothers and turn from the law to the right or to the left. Then he and his descendants will reign a long time over his kingdom in Israel. (Deuteronomy 17:18-20)*

4. Meditate on the text. 'Meditate' is a loaded word for some, being associated mostly with eastern mysticism and Yoga. There the emphasis is frequently on **emptying** our minds; the objective of the kind of meditation I am talking about is to **fill** our minds, not with our own thoughts, but with God's.

The core idea is simple: to chew the text over, like a cow chewing the cud, to read and re-read, to let each individual word or phrase swirl around in our head so that we taste every part of the text. Psalm 119 – a fantastic Psalm to fire us up about God's Word – talks of meditation in this healthy sense.

> *"Oh, how I love your law! I mediate on it all day long. Your commands make me wiser than my enemies, for they are ever with me. I have more insight than all my teachers, for I meditate on your statues." (Psalm 119:97-99)*

Try doing this with individual verses, or very short passages. For example, from Philippians, try meditating on these statements from Chapter 2:

"If you have any encouragement from being united with Christ, if any comfort from his love, if any fellowship with the Spirit, if any tenderness and compassion, then make my joy complete by being like-minded, having the same love, being one in spirit and purpose." (Philippians 2:1,2)

Savour each word or phrase, read it over and over again emphasising a different word or phrase each time; let your mind dwell on it, let the words inspire your imagination.

5. Memorise. Psalm 119:11 contains these famous words: "I have hidden your word in my heart that I might not sin against you." Something of the same idea is contained in Paul's statement: "Let the word of Christ dwell in your heart richly" (Colossians 3:16).

Memorising Scripture might be a daunting prospect for some. It may not be something you have ever done. On the other hand, it may be something with rather negative associations which you would prefer to leave behind in your childhood. In addition many would say – and I'm discovering it to be true - that the older they get the harder it becomes to remember where you left your Bible, let alone to memorise it!

Meditation is a key to memorisation. I have rarely sat down deliberately to memorise any particular Scripture verse – except in my childhood, and only then for financial reward! I have found, however, that repeated reading and meditating on the same text has often resulted in that text sticking in my mind.

As we hide God's truth in our hearts this way, it is quite remarkable how often these statements come back to mind just when they are needed – to encourage, to warn, to provide a guiding principle. Of course, if the statements were never hidden in our hearts in the first place it will be very difficult to find them when we need them.

Here are some statements from Philippians Chapter 1 which would make excellent verses for meditation and memory:

1:6 "Being confident of this, that he who began a good work in you will carry it on to completion until the day of Christ Jesus."

1:9-11 "And this is my prayer: that your love may abound more and more in knowledge and depth of insight, so that you may be able to discern what is best and may be pure and blameless until the day of Christ, filled with the fruit of righteousness that comes through Jesus Christ – to the glory and praise of God."

1:21 "For to me, to live is Christ and to die is gain."

1:27 "Whatever happens, conduct yourselves in a manner worthy of the gospel of Christ."

1:29 "For it has been granted to you on behalf of Christ not only to believe on him, but also to suffer for him..."

You may notice that these verses are not simply the type of statements which will provide us with warm feelings when life is getting us down. Some of course will. But they will do more than that. The impact of Scripture on our lives, according to Paul includes "teaching, rebuking, correcting and training in righteousness" (2 Timothy 3:16). Since we have to be selective in our Scripture memory – unless we learn whole books - we should select those statements which taken together will feed this transformation in our lives, rather than provide us with an unbalanced, feel-good factor.

You may come up with other more creative ways of connecting with the words of Scripture. The important thing is not the method, it is the reality of contact with God's Word in a way that leads to the renewal of our thinking and thus to life transformation. We are not to be conformed to the thinking, the beliefs, the values of this present age. We are not to allow the world to squeeze us into its mould. Rather, we are to be transformed by the renewing of our mind.[2]

[2] Romans 12:1, 2

Our motivation in coming to Scripture is **first and foremost to know Christ,** to encounter him through the Word. It is possible to know the Bible inside out, it is possible to study theology, and yet not to know Christ. It is possible on the other hand that we may struggle continually in our attempts to study the Bible and yet know Christ deeply. This is our primary aim, and indeed nowhere is it better expressed than by Paul in Philippians 3:10,11:

"I want to know Christ and the power of his resurrection and the fellowship of sharing in his sufferings, becoming like him in his death, and so, somehow, to attain to the resurrection from the dead."

Our **second** prime motivation is that **Scripture will mould and shape us to become more like Christ.** We are not simply reading the Bible for information, but also for **formation** – our desire is that it will form and transform us by the power of God's Spirit. It follows then that our focus is not primarily on quantity – how much of the Bible we get through – but on quality – how much of the Bible gets through us!

Some tourists think they have 'done France' simply by spending a day in Paris. Ours is not the approach of the tourist, but of the citizen. Our citizenship, Paul tells us in Philippians 3, is in heaven – we want to breathe its air, we want to explore its glories, we want to understand its culture. It is not just about how much we see, but how deep we go. "We can read in such a way that the words go through our brains but don't find their way into our hearts."[3]

[3] Mel Lawrenz, op cit, p 63

We read God's Word not simply so that we master the text, but so that the text will master us. General, informational reading of Scripture is important so that we know the main characters and events, and can follow the story line of the Bible. But for life change to occur, we must go deeper. Sadly, for many people, reading the Bible is little more than another item on their 'to do' list which they get over with.

Reading that transforms takes time.

"Often we are so burdened and overwhelmed with other thoughts, images and concerns that it may take a long time before God's Word has swept all else aside and come through.... This is the very reason why we begin our meditation with

the prayer that God may send His Holy Spirit to us through His Word and reveal His Word to us and enlighten us." [4]

We need to come to our reading both thoughtfully and **responsively.** As Bonhoeffer underlines, we must come open and responsive to God, dependent upon him, anticipating that his Spirit will speak through the Word into our lives. And as we read, we take the position of the learner, the servant, not seeking to judge God's Word, nor to pick and choose what we happen to like from it, disregarding the rest, but rather seeking to let God's Word judge us and shape our life according to his agenda.

"Pride, prejudice and preconceptions are the big barrier to seeing truth. Be humble. Look at what is there. Tell God you know your mind has limitations. Thank him that he will help you understand." [5]

We need to learn to respond.

RESPONSIVE READING

What might this mean at a practical level? Here is a short section from Chapter 2 of Philippians:

If therefore there is any encouragement in Christ, if there is any consolation of love, if there is any fellowship of the Spirit, if any affection and compassion, make my joy complete by being of the same mind, maintaining the same love, united in spirit, intent on one purpose.
Do nothing from selfishness or empty conceit, but with humility of mind let each of you regard one another as more important than himself; do not merely look out for your own personal interests, but also for the interests of others.
Have this attitude in yourselves which was also in Christ Jesus, who, although He existed in the form of God, did not regard equality with God a thing to be grasped, but emptied Himself, taking the form of a bond-servant, and being made in the likeness of men. And being found in appearance as a man, He humbled Himself by becoming obedient to the point of death, even death on a cross. Therefore also God highly exalted Him, and bestowed on Him the name which is above every name, that at the name of Jesus every knee should bow, of those who are in heaven, and on earth, and under the earth, and that every tongue should confess that Jesus Christ is Lord, to the glory of God the Father.

There are at least three different ways in which we can turn a passage of Scripture like this into **responsive reading.**

1. First of all, as we read the passage, we can respond by **thanking God.** For example, we could pause to thank him for the good things which are part of our experience of Christ: encouragement from being joined to Christ, comfort from his love, fellowship with the Spirit. Whatever our circumstances right now, we can still

[4] Dietrich Bonhoeffer, Life Together, New York, Harper & Row, 1956, pp 82-83

[5] John White, The Fight, Inter-varsity Press, 1977, p 45

thank God for these things. They are true. What is more, as we think about them, their reality might fill us in a new way and they might begin to impact our experience.

2. A second kind of response is to use the exhortation Paul makes (and through him the Holy Spirit) as a **trigger to our prayer life.** Often, frankly, our praying is shallow, self-centred and repetitive. Turning Scripture into the fuel on which our prayers feed is very enriching. For example, with this passage in Philippians in mind, we could pray that we might bring joy to the Lord's heart by developing a like-mindedness with the believers we know; by growing in our love for them; we could ask the Holy Spirit to sift through our motivation so that those things that are driven by selfishness are removed; we could pray specifically regarding how we might encourage and help others in what they are doing.

3. A third kind of response is that of **adoration and worship.** The final paragraph is one of the best known in the Bible, for good reason. Read the paragraph through several times. Let the portrait it paints of the Lord Jesus fill your mental vision and fire your imagination. Don't let the truth wash over you - let it wash through you. Respond to it in your mind and heart - even out loud if you like. Respond to him.

In these three ways our reading has **a two-way dimension** which can lift it to another level. There is encounter with God here.

Not every part of Philippians or any other book for that matter will lend itself so readily to this kind of responsive reading. But if we make this a regular habit, it will enrich our relationship with Christ.

Whatever the nature of the text, whatever the form of the study, we need to come with the desire and expectation of encountering God and of hearing his voice. David's prayer is so appropriate: "Open my eyes that I might see wonderful things in your law." (Psalm 119:18) Attitude is key. Remember that this is not a summons from our Bank Manager - it is a love letter from our Creator.

THE RESPONSE OF OBEDIENCE

There is, of course, a fourth kind of response, without which our Bible reading will achieve little. This is the **response of obedience.**

There are all kinds of voices in the world clamouring for our attention. **There is only one voice that values us enough to give his life for us.** Jesus is the Good Shepherd who lays down his life for the sheep. No other voice will give us the sense of personal value and significance that he will give. The three disciples who witnessed the transfiguration of Jesus came back down to earth with these words from heaven ringing in their ears: "This is my Son. Listen to him."[6]

[6] Matthew 17:5

We are not simply bringing our mind to Scripture to try to understand it. We are not simply bringing our heart to Scripture to respond to the love of God. We are bringing our will, our plans, our ambitions, our lifestyle and values, our motives and goals - and we are submitting them all to the voice of our Lord.

Disciples of Jesus Christ are not merely learners in a theoretical, academic sense. They are apprentices, learner-practitioners. They submit to and apply what they learn, modelling their lives on their Master. They follow their teacher – that is what is implied by 'listening'. In fact, Jesus warned us to be careful how we hear. For hearing makes us responsible. We are hearing divine truth, not human opinion. We have a response to make.

Often, if we are honest with ourselves, our problems with Scripture have little to do with a lack of understanding of what is being said to us. The problem is that we understand only too well! We can see what it means, and what it means implies correction, sometimes uncomfortable and costly change. "If you continue in my word, then you are truly disciples of mine; and you will know the truth, and the truth will make you free."[7]

[7] John 8:31, 32

There is nothing automatic here. Continuing in his word – learning and living it – will indicate that we are true disciples. As we do that we will know the truth and this truth will liberate us. But apart from obedience, there is no experiencing truth-that-sets-free. The person who claims to be interested to find out what truth is, but who has no intention of actually living according to truth, will never discover it. God is not interested in playing games with us.

4 BIBLE MAPPING

The basic approach we are following is likely to be rather different from what you might have thought, or even what you may have followed before. Our approach in the study of an individual book of the Bible is to **grasp the big picture first** and then gradually to narrow the focus.

This does not sit well with our natural impatience! And other approaches may appear to offer much more, much sooner. Yet we need to be a little wary of methods of Bible study that either claim or give the impression that after ten minutes or so we will have a guaranteed experience of hearing God speak. Indeed, the real danger is that, without a grasp of the book as a whole, our understanding of individual statements and passages can easily end up being superficial at best and faulty at worst.

We need a general framework, an overall structure to enable us to grasp the significance of the individual pieces. Just as the individual parts of a car may be of interest to some, but they make very little sense divorced from their function within the framework of the whole vehicle, so the individual parts of a text will make little sense to most of us if considered in isolation from their context. So rather than plunge into line by line, word by word study, we have begun by reading, re-reading and again re-reading the whole letter, in order to grasp the big picture.

If you are anything like me, however, even after reading the letter twelve times (let alone three or four), you may find it difficult to retain even the major ingredients of the letter in your mind, especially if the letter is completely new to you. You may feel the way an explorer feels upon discovering a fascinating new island: excitement at the new discovery, and yet overwhelmed by so much new material. What we need is a way to bring some order to what we have encountered, to map out the new territory so that we can begin to appreciate its basic shape and contours. So one of the first exercises we should do as we re-read the text, is to **make ourselves a 'map' of the key content.**

Maps are very useful – for tourists, for sales personnel, for planners, for military strategists, for all of us who need to find our way around a city or country. The kind of map I am going to suggest in this unit is a helpful tool in finding our way around a text.

Many years ago, the great thinker Aristotle pointed out that a work of literature – as distinct from some of the essays I wrote in school - has a beginning, a middle and an end. Rather than being a random collection of unconnected thoughts, there is direction, movement and shape. The text goes somewhere, and as we study it we seek to follow its journey.

The discipline of making a map helps us at least to begin to see this movement, to see how we get from one place to the next. It helps to introduce us to the key concept of **thought flow**, to which we will return in much greater detail. It will help us to see at a glance not only what the key issues are, but also what themes are repeated, and where; what the balance or proportion of a particular issue is to the whole letter. And of course it shows us where we have been; it acts as a short-hand reminder of what we have discovered so far.

The map therefore is designed to be a working document to which we will return again and again as we seek to grasp the meaning and message of the letter.

This is probably a rather unfamiliar exercise for most and it is worth thinking about for a moment before you start. How much do we put into our map of Philippians? How should we set it out?

Keep the following in mind:

- the idea is to produce something that is of practical use to you, not something which is a work of art!

- maps are deliberately **selective** – they don't show every rock, nor even every bend in the road unless they are very large scale. They give the major details that are required in order for us to be able to see at a glance how the land lies.

- we don't start with the finished article – the map will be added to and revised constantly as we go through. Some things that we miss first time round we will eventually see and have to add; some things that seemed of primary importance in our first walks through the terrain will give place to other things that we come to see as having greater strategic value in the text.

- so - **don't worry too much about 'getting it right'**.

How should we set out our 'map'?

It could be done as a 'table of contents' – set out entirely in words in the form of headings, summary statements, key phrases and words, as in our first example. This is probably the most straightforward way of doing it, especially for those who, like me, are artistically challenged and would not do well with real maps! And since the object is to have a practical, working document and not a work of art, this should suffice. (See sample map #1)

However, it has to be said that this approach lacks in imagination! More seriously, many of us think much more in terms of pictures rather than in abstract concepts, and having a graphical dimension to our 'map' can be of great benefit in helping us to both crystallise our thinking and remember what the key issues are – not to mention that it is much more fun! So adding stick figures, symbols and even colour bring more corners of our brain into action and can serve to make the whole exercise much more meaningful, memorable and enjoyable. (See sample maps #2& 3)

CHAPTER AND VERSE

The edition of the Bible you are using already has a number of 'helps' in order to make it easier to find the way around:

- there is a table of contents at the start

- the book divisions are clearly marked

- each book is divided up into chapters and verses.

As you make out your table of contents you need to bear in mind that **the chapter and verse divisions in our versions of the Bible were not part of the original text**. They were added much later. They are, of course, a great help in finding our way quickly to a specific part in the text – especially as page numbering varies from one edition to the next - but they can sometimes make the books of the Bible look as if they consist of a series of disconnected statements, rather than a flow of narrative.

It is much more helpful, therefore, to think in terms of **paragraphs** rather than in terms of individual verses. If you are reading the New International Version (the version I will be using throughout this guide) you will find that in addition to chapters and verses, the text is divided into paragraphs. It is helpful to **follow these paragraphs** as you map out the contents, at least until you are more familiar with the text.

In addition, the NIV divides each book into **sections** and gives each section a short title (in italics to show it is not part of the original text) which sums up its content. These can be useful, or they can get in the way. It would certainly stimulate your mind more if you decide for yourself what each unit of thought is about.

As you set out either your table or map of contents, try where possible to **use key words from the text itself**. This will prevent you from rushing too quickly to the interpretation stage. It will also help later when you are looking for repeated ideas, words and themes.

Since this is an unfamiliar exercise the next pages contain two examples of a Bible map. The first is in the form of a Table of Contents, the second is more of a graphical representation of the text. There is lots of room for variation and improvement, but these are offered simply to get you started.

You will notice that the examples are incomplete, focussing only on the final chapter of Philippians. Feel free to use them in whatever way and combination you wish, but you will have to complete the map for the first three chapters!

PHILIPPIANS 4 - TABLE OF CONTENTS

Sample Map #1

1-9   **The peace of God and the God of peace**

Appeal to two workers to agree with each other - request to fellow-worker to help

Presenting requests to God: God's peace guarding our hearts and minds

Thinking about the right things and living Paul's example: the God of peace with us

10-20   **The secret of contentment**

Joy: their concern for Paul

Contentment in every situation – through Christ who gives strength

The Philippians' giving to Paul – repeated – financial gifts as a pleasing and acceptable sacrifice to God

God supplies all need according to his riches in Christ

21-23   **The personal touch**

Greetings to and from everyone - especially those from Caesar's household

Note that in the interests of brevity and clarity in the above example I sometimes depart from the words of the text of Philippians, particularly to give summary statements. You may prefer not to do this. The point is to have a **usable document**, not a series of fancy headings.

PHILIPPIANS 4 – MAP OF CONTENTS

Sample Map #2

PHILIPPIANS 4 – MAP OF CONTENTS

Sample Map #3

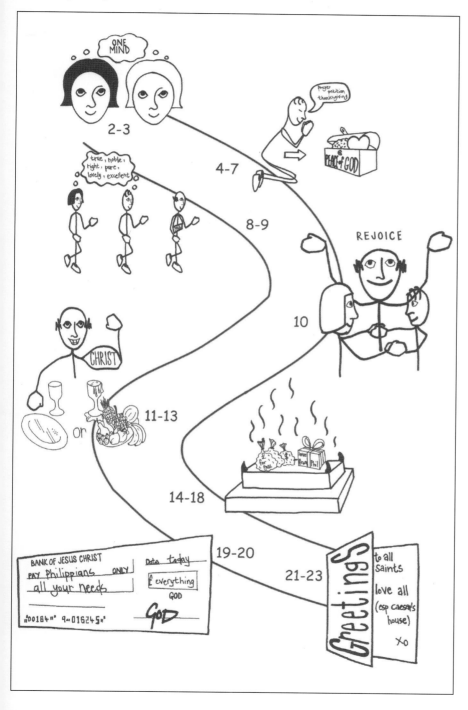

IT'S YOUR TURN!

So, now, over to you! **Read** the letter through again, and **map out the contents.**

It is best to do this on one, or at the most two sheets of paper – Philippians has only four chapters – so that you can survey the entire contents of the book at a glance, without having to turn pages in the process.

As you do this mapping exercise, not only will you become more familiar with the letter as a whole, but also the major themes and emphases will begin to emerge more clearly.

QUESTIONS

We have now read through Philippians sufficiently to have a good grasp of its content. We have made our own map – the shape of this new territory is beginning to come clear. We know what is in it, but perhaps not what it all means, nor why it needed to be written, nor how it applies to us. So, what now?

We are not yet at the point of engaging in a detailed verse by verse study, even though you may be positively itching to do so!

Patience. Remember our basic principle of approach: **start with the big picture and then gradually narrow our focus.**

ASKING THE RIGHT QUESTIONS

According to Aristotle, **the person who succeeds is the person who asks the right questions.**

There are at least two major kinds of questions that children ask almost as soon as they can talk. **What?** questions and **why?** questions. It is the mark of a healthy child to be curious.

Many a car journey in our family has been accompanied by an incessant stream of questioning:

"What's that, daddy?"

"It's a car transporter, son."

"What's a car transporter?"

"It is a big truck that carries cars."

"What does it do?"

"It carries cars to car showrooms."

"What's a car showroom?"

 "It's a place where you can buy a car."

Fun stuff.

Rather more taxing are the **why?** or the **so what?** questions:
    "Why do you shave, daddy?"
    "To cut off the hair that grows on my face."
    "Why?"
    "Because it gets scratchy if I don't cut it."
    "But why does it grow?"
    "It just grows."
    "Why do I not shave?"
    "Because you are a girl?"
    "Why do girls not shave?"
    "Well..."

Sadly what sometimes happened was that, worn down by the incessant barrage of questions, I would finally grind out "Because I say so!" with sufficient vehemence that the poor child didn't ask any more questions - at least for two minutes.

The key to learning is first **to ask questions**, and then to learn **to ask the right questions.** Unfortunately, well before we have left our teens, many of us either give up our God-given curiosity or have it driven out of us.

The most useful and important questions that we will ask when it comes to investigating Scripture are **what?** and **why?**

The first exercise we have done has been to answer the basic what? question: what is this book about? At least, we have started to answer it. We have a good idea of the major content but we are not yet at the point where we could stand up and with confidence say "Paul's purpose in writing Philippians was to..." This takes us beyond the what? question to consider why it was that this particular content was written to this particular church at this particular time.

THE BIG QUESTION

Let's start with perhaps the most basic **why?** question: **why did Paul write Philippians?**

We could put our question a different way: **would it matter if Philippians were left out of the New Testament?** Would it really matter if we somehow lost Philippians? Would we not be able to teach its message perfectly well from other letters Paul wrote?

The fundamental assumption of our approach in this guide is that Philippians is part of the New Testament and the New Testament is part of 'Scripture' – it is part of God's writing to us, part of God's revelation of himself to us. Like all good teachers, God repeats things! But is Philippians simply a repetition of what is said elsewhere, or has it a particular message that no other book communicates in quite the same way? We are going to proceed on the assumption that **Philippians has something particular and unique to tell us** and part of our task is to find out what that is.

The answer to this particular **why?** question may come under two different headings:

- the **historical occasion** of the letter – that is, the particular set of circumstances that led to the letter being written

- the **spiritual occasion** of the letter – what are the key and urgent spiritual issues that the writer is seeking to address?

The two often combine, at least at some point. We will find Paul using the historical circumstances - such as his need to explain when he is coming to visit, or his desire to say thank you for a gift - as an opportunity to deal with some deeper spiritual issues which he knows the church (or the individual) needs to hear about at this time.

DOES IT MATTER WHAT THE AUTHOR INTENDED?

It has become fashionable in recent years, and not just in academic circles, virtually to discount the author's intention when it comes to how we interpret a text, even if the author makes his or her intention clear. For we cannot really know what the author's intention was, (and especially not if he lived 2000 years or more ago). Moreover we must not allow any author, ancient or modern, to impose his meaning upon us. What matters is not what the author had in mind, but what we have in mind as we read. The text is all there is. The author is dead, long live the reader.

Many no longer believe that there is any objective meaning in texts which we as readers should seek out with all our ability, using agreed interpretive technique, and to which we as readers should submit. Each of us creates our own meaning, imposes our own interpretation upon the text as we interact with it. What matters is not what the text means, but **what the text means to me**. Thus there is no such thing as 'the right interpretation'. There are just opinions, and each opinion is as valid (or invalid) as the next.

To deal thoroughly with this approach is beyond the scope of this guide[1] but it is important to be at least aware of it because sooner or later we will come across it, if we haven't already. It comes across in such commonly heard statements as, "It's just a matter of opinion what the Bible means"; or "You can make the Bible mean whatever you want it to mean"; or "That might work for you, but it means something different to me."

For the moment – and we will return to this at other points in this guide - two observations are important:

[1] For a detailed treatment of this issue see Kevin J Vanhoozer, Is there a meaning in this text?, Apollos, 1998

- at the immediate level, most of us instinctively understand that letters are normally written with a purpose or purposes which the authors usually make clear. They are intended to communicate a message. To ignore clear authorial intention is virtually a guarantee that we will end up making the letter mean what it never could have meant. No meaningful written communication would be possible. Why, according to this theory, I could even interpret a letter from my bank manager warning me that I am badly overdrawn as an invitation to spend more!

- at a deeper level, behind the biblical author is the 'breath of God', the Holy Spirit. The Bible is not simply a collection of literature, it is divine communication. God has the clear intention of revealing himself, of letting us know his will, through the Scriptures. He has not let loose a text into the world as some mystery object to whose meaning there are no sure clues. If he has, then the sure knowledge of God through his Word is impossible.

Understanding authorial intention is a vital ingredient to the accurate interpretation of the Bible.

DOES THE WRITER TELL US WHY HE IS WRITING?

It is particularly helpful if the biblical authors tell us in very specific terms why they are writing. Some do. For example Luke tells us right at the beginning of his Gospel why he is writing:

> *Inasmuch as many have undertaken to compile an account of the things accomplished among us, just as those who from the beginning were eyewitnesses and servants of the word have handed them down to us, it seemed fitting for me as well, having investigated everything carefully from the beginning, to write it out for you in consecutive order, most excellent Theophilus;* **so that you might know the exact truth about the things you have been taught.** *(Luke 1:1-2:52 Emphasis added)*

Some other biblical writers make us read much further into their work before telling us explicitly what their purpose is. In his first letter John gives a number of reasons for writing. For example, "I write this to you so that you will not sin" (1 John 2:1). Where the writer is explicit like this in telling us why he is writing it is very helpful, for we can then read and study the entire book, or individual sections of the book, in light of the stated purpose.

Consider this from towards the end of John's Gospel:

> *Jesus did many other miraculous signs in the presence of his disciples, which are not recorded in this book. But these are written that you may believe that Jesus is the Christ, the Son of God, and that by believing you may have life in his name. (John 20:30, 31)*

Here John explains the purpose of his gospel – or more exactly, the purpose that lies behind his choice of signs from among the many miracles Jesus performed. There is nothing arbitrary in his choice, for example, of the changing of water into wine, the healing of the government official's son and the raising of Lazarus. He is not simply listing supernatural events. He calls the miracles 'signs', for they are miracles with a message - miracles which have been deliberately selected as signposts to the identity of Jesus as Messiah and Son of God.

How do they do that? That is the point! Arriving at an answer to that question will go a long way towards helping us to understand the particular message of the fourth gospel.

Not all biblical authors are as kind to us as John! They do not always tell us so explicitly why they are writing, so we have to dig deeper to find an answer.

What about Philippians?

Spend a few minutes looking over your table of contents, and perhaps re-read Philippians with this 'why?' question in mind. Then write out what seems to you to be the answer to the question. You may uncover a number of major purposes. In that case write them all down.

Just do it! (Before going on to the next page.)

What did you find?

You probably didn't find any sentence beginning: "I am writing this because..." So we need to look a little more closely.

Perhaps one indication comes in 1:12: "Now I want you to know brothers, that what has happened to me has really served to advance the gospel."

Phrases such as "I want you to know" are a frequent indication of purpose. In this particular case, Paul's imprisonment had clearly caused a mixed reaction amongst the believers, as the subsequent verses explain. Some were inspired by it, emboldened to go out themselves and bring the good news to others, knowing the real reason for Paul's incarceration: the defence of the gospel. Others, however, were motivated by envy and rivalry. They were secretly glad that Paul was in prison. In fact, some of them were probably saying that it was his own fault, and that if he really had been doing God's will, if God had truly been with him, this would never have happened to him. (Christians can be so encouraging!)

What would the Philippians have felt when they heard the news? Paul had brought many of them to faith. They had experienced what it was like to have Paul in prison in their own city, but on that occasion God had brought about a miraculous and almost immediate release. Not this time. Could it really be God's will for Paul to be kept inside? Or was this person who had established their church proving to be of questionable character? Had he deceived them? Was the money they were sending him a waste of resources?

It might be fair to think that here lies a very practical reason for writing the letter: to tell the concerned folks at Philippi what exactly was happening to him, how he felt about it and how he saw the future, so that rather than being discouraged by his imprisonment, they would have all the more boldness to get on with the job of communicating the Gospel. And indeed he talks very much in these terms, particularly in Chapter 1.

Have you found other potential reasons for writing?

Perhaps you have considered the references to Timothy and to Epaphroditus in Chapter 2: "I hope in the Lord Jesus to send Timothy to you soon..." "I think it is necessary to send back to you Epaphroditus... whom you sent to take care of my needs. For he longs for all of you and is distressed because you heard he was ill." Here are more reasons for writing – to pass on this basic information regarding the two men.

Perhaps your attention has been taken by Chapter 3 and its references to **'dogs'**, to **'enemies of the cross'**. Could it be that the real reason for writing - or at least one of the reasons - was to warn the Philippians about these people, whoever they were? To tell them how to recognise them and to explain the dangers they posed?

Or is this letter basically a rather lengthy way of saying thank you to the Philippians for their financial support? (See Chapter 4)

So we have several candidates for answers to our question – and there are doubtless a few more. And all of them may well be right in the sense that Paul may have had a number of important purposes for writing his letter. But – and this is the key question - **can we discern a major overall purpose**, the distinctive message and application of this short letter? Paul has made our quest a little more challenging than perhaps we had hoped!

THE STORY SO FAR

What we have succeeded in doing so far, however, is first of all to become acquainted with the basic content of his letter. Secondly, we have started to penetrate beneath the surface of the letter. We have read it one more time, but this time with a purpose in mind. And this is very important, particularly, as we have seen, for those of us whose minds are prone to wander. Most of us find it much easier to concentrate if there is a story, but Philippians is one of those parts of the Bible which give lots of detail, but little in the way of story line.

In the absence of a plot, we are like a murder detective in a room which is full of clues but which has no body. We need to begin to piece the evidence together, to find out what the clues are telling us. Indeed, some of the things in the room may not seem at all like clues when we begin. It will only be after we have unearthed a vital piece of information that suddenly we will begin to see certain things in a different light.

We have asked one simple question of our material, but already we have started to penetrate the mystery. It is far from clear yet, but at least we have begun.

The next few chapters are designed to help us dig deeper still in the hope that the major message of Philippians will begin to emerge.

6 THE DIAGNOSIS

I have a vivid memory of a series of visits to the dentist. My weekly diet of a large bag of old fashioned boiled sweets (we are talking 40 years ago!) clearly did not help matters, and with various unexplained twinges in my mouth I went for a check up. My affable old dentist peered around in the dark through his half moon glasses and pronounced with satisfaction that my teeth were sound. My delight at this unexpected escape was mixed with twinge-induced doubt.

Sure enough, my mouth did not agree with his verdict, so some weeks later I took myself to another dentist. He had some strange new gadgets including an x-ray machine (and no glasses). When the x-rays of my teeth were processed it was discovered that I needed no fewer than eleven fillings and one extraction. (It's sometimes tempting to prefer ignorance!)

Making a diagnosis is one of the most helpful ways of approach to the letters in the New Testament because **each of them is dealing with a diseased situation** of one kind or another. Each of the New Testament letters is written against the background of particular difficulties, dangers and spiritual diseases. Paul and the other writers are not simply passing the time of day. There is nothing accidental or superfluous in their writing. They are writing with God's answer to their particular problems, God's treatment and cure for their particular disease. If we are going to understand the cure, the treatment prescribed - and apply it to ourselves appropriately - we will need to understand the diagnosis.

A good doctor will take time over the diagnosis. Appearances – as in the case of my teeth – can be deceptive. A series of tests will be run to ascertain what exactly is wrong. Then a course of treatment will be prescribed. Not only that, but the doctor will also consider external factors - threats to health from the environment and lifestyle - and suggest ways in which these threats can be combated and the patient protected from catching the disease again.

WHAT APPEARS TO BE THE PROBLEM?

I'm always tempted to answer the question, "What appears to be the problem?", with "You're the doctor. You tell me!" But the doctor really does want to know how we feel. Not all symptoms are obvious and the pain or discomfort we are experiencing will (hopefully) help the doctor get to the root of the problem. We will need first to look for **symptoms.**

Then we will need to make a **diagnosis**, based on a more thorough examination. A headache could well be the result of lack of sleep. Or it might be due to deteriorating eyesight. Or it might be a symptom of something deeper, something much more sinister. A cancer, an attack on the nervous system, a major infection.

It will be clear already from our reading of Philippians that Paul was not simply looking for a way to occupy his time on a wet Sunday. There is more to his reason for picking up his pen than being bored with prison life. In the middle of all the encouraging words - and it is a wonderfully encouraging letter - there is **evidence of threats to their spiritual health**. There are symptoms that all may not be well in the church at Philippi.

Chapter 3, for example, talks about human **dogs, evil workers**, that may come against them. **External threats**. In addition, Chapter 4 mentions two fellow workers who have fallen out with each other. This clear evidence of disharmony indicates deeper spiritual disease **within** the local community of believers.

Although we may be strongly tempted to rush to the 'how can I apply this to my life?' stage, we should remind ourselves that when it comes to issues of our own health, we are very glad when the consultants take the time for a thorough examination before arriving at their diagnosis. The more time they take, the more confidence we tend to have in the accuracy of their diagnosis.

The same is true when it comes to matters of spiritual health: we need to take time to take all symptoms into account and to probe deeper causes. A correct diagnosis is vital, otherwise it is highly probable that the wrong treatment will be prescribed.

Here we have the decided advantage that the Holy Spirit, through Paul, will prescribe the cure for us. However, we might miss the cure altogether, or at least its significance, **if we don't first of all identify what the disease is that he is seeking to cure**. Moreover, we should remember that one particular treatment will not deal with every disease. It is likely that there was more than one problem amongst the believers at Philippi, needing more than one solution.

MAKING OUR DIAGNOSIS

Let's approach the letter, then, as a consultant would a patient. We want to look first of all at the **symptoms**, including both positive and negative health indicators. The news is rarely all bad, and when a patient is having to face up to the fact that something is seriously wrong, it can be very encouraging to find out that something is right as well!

Then we need to look for possible **causes** and explanations particularly for the negative symptoms. Here it might be helpful to look at two main areas:

- external conditions that might be affecting their health – for example financial pressures, persecution, false teachers: look particularly at the factual detail he gives about experiences, people, events, social conditions

- personal weaknesses – for example, lack of understanding, ingrained sin, personality issues, individual or group psychology: look particularly for terms that indicate spiritual struggle, psychological condition (states of fear or anxiety, for example).

To do this with Philippians - yes, you've guessed it - we will need to read the letter through again.

Read each chapter carefully, asking all the time questions like these:

- why does Paul need to say this?

- is there anything he appears to repeat or emphasise?

- what does this information reveal about their spiritual condition?

- is there an underlying problem here that I haven't picked up on?

- is there any indication as to why they are experiencing what they are experiencing?

Take some time - NOW - to do this. On the next page you will find a simple 'chart' on which to set out the symptoms (positive and negative), and on the following page an opportunity to set out the negative symptoms together with their possible underlying causes as revealed by the text. Rather than write in this guide you may choose to photocopy the pages , or rule out your own, as worksheets.

You might find that this particular exercise is better done as a group activity – it would certainly be more fun.

The Symptoms

Positive	Negative

Now work on the second area, that of **possible causes.**

The Causes

Negative symptom	Possible cause

Main external influences noticed:

CONSULTANT'S SUMMARY

On the basis of the symptoms you have noted, and the possible causes you have found, it is now time to write up your diagnosis. Don't include a suggested treatment or cure at this stage. (You may choose to photocopy this page as a worksheet.)

I do hope you are not cheating! If you have reached this page without working through the diagnosis of Philippians for yourself, you are!

I can't slap you over the wrist for it, but from your point of view, what you have done is to deny yourself the experience of working through the process - which effectively will defeat the objective of this guide.

Now that you have worked through the process for yourself, let me give you some reflections that came from my own attempt at a diagnosis. Again this will not be exhaustive, but it might be useful for me to go through part of the process with you so that you get a feel for the sort of questions that I would tend to ask.

Positive	
The Holy Spirit highlights certain very positive features about the spiritual health of these folks. In fact the letter begins and ends with symptoms of encouraging spirituality. They are commended for their partnership with Paul in the work of communicating the gospel (1:5). This is strong evidence, according to Paul, that God has begun a good work in them, and having begun he is committed to finishing what he started. It is their partnership with him which is stressed again at the end (4:10 -20). This time it is the financial nature of their sharing with him which is mentioned - in fact they stand out as being the only church to be involved in supporting Paul in this way. Another positive feature is that they are clearly a responsive church - at least they were when Paul was with them, and he reminds them of this (2:12). They started to work their salvation out in everyday living - now he encourages them to continue this process even as God continues his work in them. And they are no strangers to the concept of sacrifice, of service to God and to Paul which is costly to them (1:29; 2:17; 4:18), to the extent of physical suffering. The individuals which Paul mentions by name are clearly hard-working people, whatever their other faults: genuine believers who are prepared for work for their Lord.	

How does this compare with your assessment of their symptoms of spiritual health? I'm sure you have noticed a few other things. Is there any evidence, for example, that they were a praying church? Keep your additional ideas in mind as we move on.

The Negative

Turning to the negative side and the indications of spiritual weakness, disease or danger, here are two symptoms and possible underlying causes which we could note at this stage.

Negative symptom	Possible cause
Symptom: one of the clearest symptoms of disease comes in Chapter 4 where two Christian co-workers have fallen out with each other. The indications are that this situation was causing anxiety and disturbing the peace of other believers (4:6-9). The exhortations at the beginning of Chapter 2 may have been given with this in mind. In particular, it may explain the emphasis on working together, on fellow-workers and on partnership.	Cause: the immediate cause might well be a conflict that has arisen in the context of their work for the Lord. (This happens!) But disagreement does not necessarily lead to conflict. It is likely, therefore, that there are other underlying causes such as wrong attitudes (see list at start of Chapter 2) to one another, and wrong motivations (see Chapter 3) that emerge often in pressure situations in Christian service.
Symptom: a crisis of confidence is strongly indicated in Chapter 1. It would appear that their confidence had been shaken by circumstances. Paul takes pains to express his own confidence in God's work both in them, in himself and even in those who are causing him difficulty.	Cause: three main immediate causes: first, Paul's imprisonment that has come about in the course of his work for Christ (1:12-14); second, what some other Christian workers were saying about his imprisonment (1:15-18); third, opposition and persecution of some kind (1:28) which they were all facing. Paul's physical absence from them may have been having a negative psychological impact - see also 1:27 and 2:12. Once again, difficult external circumstances do not of themselves necessarily produce a crisis of confidence. It is likely that they had misplaced their confidence, had wrong or unrealistic expectations regarding the 'success' of Christian service and the spread of the gospel.

TAKING FIVE

We have come quite a long way.

Our first task was to familiarise ourselves with the text, in particular through reading and re-reading and through constructing a table of contents.

Our second task was to begin to discern the main focus and message of Philippians. The diagnosis exercise in particular has helped us to get beneath the surface of the content and certain themes have begun to emerge.

We have noted, for example, the emphasis on working together, on unity and in this context the particular problem at Philippi of two co-workers who are in conflict with each other. At the same time we have noted positive features of the church – their partnership with Paul in the spread of the gospel, their financial support for him in his service for the Lord.

It is at least possible, therefore, that the core message of Philippians might have a significant connection with service, with work for the Lord particularly in the communication and spread of the Gospel, not as isolated individuals but as a community, a fellowship of believers. As a result there is a particular focus on some of the things that can go wrong in Christian work and how either to avoid these problems, or to resolve them.

We will need more in the way of evidence from the text in order either to confirm or deny or refine these findings. So in this unit we are going to complete five more tasks which will help us continue to build up a picture of the core issues of the letter, and help us come closer to a definitive statement about its purpose.

Once again these tasks – apart from the first one – will involve us in re-reading the text! But each reading will be for a different purpose, looking for different information.

You may find working through these tasks in a group, or with one other person, to be more rewarding than working on your own – and you can hold each other accountable for not jumping ahead and reading my own suggestions which follow before working it through for yourself.

OUTLINING THE TASKS

Task 1

Look for a **key in the front door.** Study the opening couple of verses of Philippians, compare them to the opening lines of some of Paul's other letters and note down anything you find of significance.

Task 2

Identify what Paul tells us in Philippians about **the person and ministry of Jesus Christ.** What aspects of his character, achievement and present work does he underline? And can you see any connection between these aspects of Christ and the problems being faced by the believers in Philippi?

In particular it is important to discover how the death of Christ is referred to. Is the emphasis on the fact that it was a sacrifice? Is the emphasis on his physical sufferings, is it on the cross – and if so what particular feature of the cross is being highlighted?

Task 3

Find all the **references to salvation** in Philippians. What does Paul say about salvation in this letter? How does it compare with what you know of what Paul teaches in other letters on this theme? Is there anything significant here? Is there anything that you have discovered in Philippians that ties in with his particular salvation emphasis?

All the books of the Bible preach the Gospel – all present a particular aspect of the Good News. Genesis, for example, through the experience in particular of Abraham, teaches us the big lesson of 'justification by faith'; at the heart of Exodus is the necessity of deliverance through the blood of the Passover Lamb; while the focus in Leviticus is on sacrifice and holiness. What is the **'Gospel according to Philippians'?**

Task 4

Make a list of **key words and concepts** which are **repeated** in this letter, and which therefore might have particular significance. (You will find the map or table of contents particularly useful here.) Again, do these connect with anything you have discovered through the first three tasks?

Task 5

Note the **major biographical references** in Philippians – the details Paul gives us about himself and about other Christians. Are these details for information only, or might they have an important connection with the main theme or themes?

Please **pause** your reading of this guide at this point and **work through the five tasks BEFORE** we work them through together.

Task 1   **Key in the front door**

Task 2   **Person and ministry of Jesus Christ**

Task 3   **Paul's teaching on salvation**

Task 4   **Repeated words and concepts**

Task 5   **Biographical references**

1. KEY IN THE FRONT DOOR

Many of the letters of the New Testament appear to start in exactly the same way: a mention of the writer or writers and his (their) credentials; a mention of those to whom the letter is written; and a Christian greeting of the 'grace, mercy and peace' variety. This pattern followed standard letter writing practice at the time.

However, compare the following:

> *Paul, an apostle of Christ Jesus by the will of God,*
> *To the saints in Ephesus, the faithful in Christ Jesus:*
> *Grace and peace to you from God our Father and the Lord Jesus Christ.*
> *(Ephesians 1:1-2)*

> *Paul, an apostle – sent not from men nor by man, but by Jesus Christ and God the Father, who raised him from the dead – and all the brothers with me, To the churches in Galatia: Grace and peace to you from God our Father and the Lord Jesus Christ, who gave himself for our sins to rescue us from the present evil age, according to the will of our God and Father, to whom be glory for ever and ever. Amen. (Galatians 1:1-5)*

They are rather different! There is the same basic structure, but beyond that there are very significant differences:

- in Ephesians Paul's focus is on the believers at Ephesus as 'the faithful in Christ'.

- in Galatians Paul begins with an insistence that his authority as an apostle does not come from men - it is not a result of some human appointment. In addition he tells his readers that Christ's purpose was to rescue them from the present evil age.

Why the differences? The answer may well relate closely to the different main themes of the two letters. Or to put it another way, where the openings of the letters differ may well be a significant pointer to the specific message of the individual letter. This is how Philippians begins:

> *Paul and Timothy, servants of Christ Jesus,*
> *To all the saints in Christ Jesus at Philippi, together with the overseers and deacons: Grace and peace to you from God our Father and the Lord Jesus Christ. (Philippians 1:1-2)*

At first sight the greeting seems very standard and unremarkable, except for the reference to **'overseers and deacons'.** What is so noteworthy about that? Well, if we check with all the other letters in the New Testament we will find that **this is the only one that is specifically addressed to overseers and deacons.**

The word 'deacon' means **'one who serves'**, and since Paul refers to himself and Timothy as servants (using the word often translated 'slave') we could say that this is **the only letter in the New Testament explicitly written by servants to servants.**

This may not appear to have much, if any significance at the moment, but we need to keep it in mind as we consider the rest of the letter, for it just may be a key to the major message.

2. THE PERSON AND MINISTRY OF CHRIST

The most important content of any Bible book is what it reveals to us about God: Father, Son, and Holy Spirit. More specifically, Hebrews tells us that God has spoken through his Son who is "the brightness of his glory and the express image of his person"[1]. God, as John 1 explains, has manifested himself in flesh[2]. The Holy Spirit, as John 16 tells us, has come to glorify Christ, to reveal him to us[3]. So in particular we should pay attention to how Philippians presents Jesus Christ. Certainly it will share some material with other parts of the New Testament, but it is very likely that we will find one or two features that are unique to this letter.

[1] Hebrews 1:3
[2] John 1:14
[3] John 16:12-16

And so it proves. When we ask this question of Philippians the answer is almost immediate and very striking, for Chapter 2 contains perhaps the most famous pen portrait of Christ, apart from Isaiah 53.

> *Your attitude should be the same as that of Christ Jesus: Who, being in very nature God, did not consider equality with God something to be grasped, but made himself nothing, taking the very nature of a servant, being made in human likeness. And being found in appearance as a man, he humbled himself and became obedient to death – even death on a cross! Therefore God exalted him to the highest place and gave him the name that is above every name, that at the name of Jesus every knee should bow, in heaven and on earth and under the earth, and every tongue confess that Jesus Christ is Lord, to the glory of God the Father. (Philippians 2:6-11)*

This is a wonderful portrait of Christ which, even in the context of our search through the letter, should make us pause and worship.

Many sermons have been preached on these words, and even whole books written. However, for the moment, let's content ourselves simply with noticing that at the heart of this portrait is the depiction of Christ as a servant who humbled himself and became obedient, even to death on a cross. Jesus, Son of God, became a voluntary slave whose obedience extended to the shame and pain of death by crucifixion.

Why would Paul focus on this? Because it is true, of course! But why does he make this his special focus in Philippians? Perhaps it is because he wants to focus our attention on the attitudes of the true Servant of God. And why that? Perhaps because in Philippians he is particularly concerned about two of God's servants who are in conflict with each other (see Chapter 4).

More than that, we have already noted that Philippians is the only book in the New Testament to explicitly state that it is **written by servants to servants.** It is the only book in the New Testament that is specifically addressed to elders and deacons as well as the members of a local church.

If we add to that the fact that in Chapter 2 he highlights the actions and attitudes of two other servants – Timothy and Epaphroditus – and that in Chapter 3 he warns about false workers and warns about those who have totally the wrong attitudes and ambitions, who are enemies of the cross, whose god is their physical appetite and who are totally earth-bound – the beginnings of a theme are emerging, something big which is tying the whole letter together: there is a **strong focus on service and being a servant.**

3. ASPECT OF SALVATION

We have probably approached our study of Philippians in the confidence that salvation is by grace through faith and has nothing to do with works (see Ephesians 2:8-9). This is strongly borne out by a key statement in Chapter 1:6: "being confident of this, that he who began a good work in you will carry it on to completion until the day of Jesus Christ."

Salvation is from God – it is totally dependent upon his initiative, his working, his ability to finish what he has started in our lives. The reference to the 'day of Jesus Christ' is further developed in Chapter 3, where we are told:

> ...our citizenship is in heaven. And we eagerly await a Saviour from there, the Lord Jesus Christ, who, by the power that enables him to bring everything under his control, will transform our lowly bodies so that they will be like his glorious body. (Philippians 3:20, 21)

Here is another aspect of salvation, what we might call the final phase: ultimate, final, total salvation including the transformation of our physical bodies is assured. Paul has tremendous confidence that the work God has started in our lives he will bring to completion. He is confident that if he dies before the final 'day of Jesus Christ' it means that he will be immediately with Christ (1:21-24). Opposition does not faze him. Part of salvation is to recognise that not only has it been granted to us to believe in Jesus, but also to suffer for him (1:29). In that suffering we can be confident that we will be saved, **"and that by God"** (1:29).

It is interesting, however, that God's saving activity in our life is described as work. God is presented as a worker in addition to the wonderful portrayal of Christ as a servant, a voluntary slave. And then we come to what is a key statement about salvation which at first sight may be something of a surprise:

> Therefore, my dear friends, as you have always obeyed – not only in my presence, but now much more in my absence – continue to work out your salvation with fear and trembling, for it is God who works in you to will and to act according to his good purpose. (Philippians 2:12, 13)

Salvation also involves work on our part. Not work **for** salvation, not work to earn it. But we are called upon to work **out** our salvation in daily living. And this is the task of a lifetime. Even Paul himself does not consider that he has 'arrived'. He constantly presses on to make further progress and he presents this attitude and ambition as one of the marks of Christian maturity (3:12-15).

In addition to developing the attitudes of the perfect servant, becoming more and more conformed both to the death and to the resurrection life of Christ (3:10,11), one of the key arenas of work and progress is that of spreading the gospel.

This becomes even clearer when we consider our fourth task.

4. REPEATED KEY WORDS AND CONCEPTS

There is a remarkable emphasis on the word **gospel** in this short letter. Paul uses the word 9 times in Philippians, the same number as in the much longer letter to the Romans. His focus is not so much on the theology of the gospel, such as we find in Romans and Galatians. That is here and is important. His focus in Philippians, however, is on the spread of the gospel. There can be little doubt that as far as Paul (and God) is concerned one of the greatest evidences of the reality of the work of God in our lives is that the Philippians (and we) become passionate fellow-workers with Paul in the work of the Gospel.

This introduces us to another repeated concept: the idea of partnership, of fellowship, of being a fellow-worker. Note these examples:

- Chapter 1:5 Fellowship in the gospel; 1:7 all partakers with me; 1:27 - stand fast in one spirit, with one soul

- Chapter 2:1 Fellowship of the Spirit; 2:2-4 same mind, same love, one accord - no faction; 2:18 rejoice with me; 2: 22 Timothy served with me; 2:25 Epaphroditus - fellow-worker, fellow-soldier

- Chapter 3:10 Fellowship of his sufferings; 3:15 take the same view; 3:17 to be imitators together of me

- Chapter 4:2 Be of the same mind; 4:3 loyal yoke-fellow, fellow workers; 4:14 fellowship in my afflictions; 4:15 fellowship in the matter of giving.

Note also the use of the word **all** - Chapter 1:4 - pray for all of you etc.

In summary, we can say that there is **significant emphasis on unity and fellowship** - especially in context of working for Christ in the communication of the Gospel.

We might also have noticed Paul's emphasis on **psychological terms**: the word 'mind' in various forms is very common:

- 1:7, 9, 10 (knowledge, discernment, approve)
- 2:2 (twice) 3, 5, 20 (like-minded)
- 3:15 (twice), 19
- 4:2, 7 (thoughts), 8 (think), 10 (thought - twice)

In addition we come across words like confidence, joy, compassion, mercy, vainglory, care, boldness.

If one of the major themes of this letter – if not the major theme – is on **working together with God and with each other in the spread of the Gospel**, the emphasis on attitudes, motivation and psychological conditions would make a great deal of sense, for the task of personal transformation is complicated enough. Placing it both in the context of a community of broken people who are all being transformed, and in the context of a community that is seeking to communicate the message of the good news to the world, makes it even more spiritually and psychologically complex.

5. BIOGRAPHICAL REFERENCES

For such a short letter, Philippians is remarkable in the amount of biographical detail it gives.

In Chapter 1 Paul tells us about his prayer life, about the circumstances surrounding his service for God, and about his conflict of desire: should he go to heaven or stay around longer for their benefit through his service? The same remarkable frankness is found again in Chapter 3 where he gives us insight into his attitudes and values before he encountered Christ and in particular his **religious zeal**. These are contrasted with what motivates him now in his life and service for Christ. And in Chapter 4 we read of his gratitude for their personal financial gift in support of him as a Christian worker.

In addition to the details he gives about himself we also read about Timothy and Epaphroditus. Once again, the focus is on their attitudes and values when it comes to Christian work and service.

These details are very interesting in themselves, but once again if Paul's focus is on Christian work and service, then giving us the examples of Timothy and Epaphroditus and letting us into a variety of aspects and circumstances of his own life as an apostle can only serve to illustrate and enhance his theme.

CONCLUSION

By this time I think we are clear enough as to at least the contours of the major issue of Philippians. **This is a letter about work and service!** It is about God the worker, working in our lives, committing himself to complete what he has started. It is about us working out what he has worked in. It is about us working together with God and with each other – elders, deacons, church members - in standing for and communicating the good news of Jesus Christ in the world. It is about looking to Jesus, the perfect servant, as our example, taking our values and attitudes from him, not being content with progress so far, but constantly pressing on in his power towards the prize and the final transformation of even our physical bodies on the day of Jesus Christ.

GETTING DOWN TO THE DETAIL

Our first priority has been to grasp the big picture, to be clear about what kind of a wood it is before we look at the individual trees. We have spent time considering Philippians as a whole letter, rather than as a series of individual statements. In addition to all the personal spiritual benefit of taking time with God's Word, three practical benefits have emerged which will help us enormously in our study of this letter:

- First, we should now have a good grasp of the **overall content** of the letter.

- Second, we have identified a number of **major emphases or themes** – those things that Paul spends most time writing about.

- Third we have discovered that there appears to be one **main theme** that ties most, if not all of the other issues together: the theme of **work** – not in the narrow sense of 'paid employment', but in the much broader sense of God's work in and through us, and our work or service for God, particularly in harmony (or disharmony!) with other believers.

This provides the **thematic unity** of the letter – the individual emphases and issues fit into it like the segments of an orange: each different, but they belong together. From Paul's opening prayer to his final thanks for their financial support, we can see how each fits together within the whole.

With this framework or context to guide us, it is time now to get down to a more detailed consideration of the letter.

THOUGHT-FLOW IS KEY

When it comes to our general conversation we can be quite haphazard and random in what we say. Some of us say the first thing that comes into our heads – whether or not it has anything to do with the general topic of conversation. However, when it comes to written communication, our general expectation is that there is a purpose, there is a point, some kind of order, even if the logic is not always apparent (or even present).

I learned a lesson here the painful way at school. I wrote what I thought was a reasonable essay on a poem. I scored six out of twenty – and the six was generous! At least a dozen times in the margins of my work the teacher had written in red: "so what, so what, so what?" His point was that there was no point in most of the things I had written – some of them were accurate observations, but they added up to nothing: they contributed nothing to my argument – in fact there was no argument, no point, no message, just a series of random comments.

Philippians, as we have already discovered, is not a haphazard collection of thoughts – there are clear purposes in the writing, there is a discernible thematic unity. Paul, trained in classical literature, in logic, in the art of presentation of ideas and argument, was not random. He is building an argument, presenting a case. Under inspiration of the God of order, the Spirit of truth, he writes what needs to be written, in the order in which it needs to be written. There is nothing accidental about Philippians.

What we are seeking to do, therefore, is to discern the steps and movements in his argument or presentation of truth. In other words, we are seeking to identify the **'thought-flow'**.

The parts of a car engine are not placed at random – at least, if it is your car, you hope that they are not. There is a clear and careful sequence – and the engine will not work unless the sequence is right. Similarly great works of classical music are divided into movements, each playing a different role in the impact and meaning of the piece as a whole. It would not do, for example, to take out the first few exciting bars of the opening movement, and place them in the middle of the second – imagine a slow, lyrical, reflective movement being harshly interrupted by what should have been the opening fanfare!

As we move through Philippians, we are travelling along a clear, carefully prepared road towards a destination. Like a good story, there is a beginning, a middle and an end. To understand it accurately we need to be able to see what these are, and how the writer gets from the beginning to the end.

What might the application of the thought-flow principle add to our understanding of the text?

Consider John Chapter 14:1,2 which contain some of the most famous, most often quoted words in the Bible:

> *Do not let your hearts be troubled. Trust in God; trust also in me. In my Father's house are many rooms; if it were not so, I would have told you. I am going there to prepare a place for you.*

They have brought comfort to millions of people for 2000 years, and rightly so. But let's ask a thought-flow question: has this statement got anything to do with what was said in the previous paragraph (remembering, of course, that the chapter and verse divisions are not part of the original text)?

When we read the previous paragraph we discover that the key issue is Peter being told in no uncertain terms that the time would very soon come when he would actually deny Christ. Given how strongly and publicly Peter disagreed with this assessment, that denial, when it came – as it did come - would certainly have a devastating impact upon him. What is the very next thing that Jesus says? "Do not let your hearts be troubled." This was not an isolated statement, unconnected with anything else. It was spoken to a man, and to a group of men, who would experience bitter, deep personal weakness and failure. Such men needed encouragement and reassurance that failure was not final.

Seeing how these words of comfort fit in with the surrounding text adds greatly to our understanding of what Jesus was saying, and to our application of it to our own lives. Jesus knows our weaknesses and failures before we do, and yet is prepared to give wonderful assurance and security to failing people.

We need, therefore, to pay attention to the connections, the links, the changes in theme, the movements in thought, noting how each ingredient connects to what came before, leads on to what follows – or where one movement of thought ends and another begins. To do this it can help us greatly to **divide the text into paragraphs**.

PARAGRAPHS AS UNITS OF THOUGHT

We have already noted that the vast majority of Bible versions follow the historic division of the text into chapters and verses. These are helpful as markers, grid references on the map so that we can physically find our way around the text. But they are frequently unhelpful as guides to the thought-flow.

As a result, many of the Bible editions divide the text up additionally into **paragraphs**, and some, like the NIV, divide it up into **sections** which often consist of a group of paragraphs. This can be very helpful in identifying key stages in the thought-flow.

Different versions of the Bible have different approaches to paragraphing. Here is a comparison of four different versions and their paragraphing of Philippians 1.

NIV	RSV	English Revised	New American SB
1-2	1-2	1-2	1-2
3-6	3-11	3-11	3-11
7-8			
9-11			
12-14	12-14	12-30	12-30
15-18		15-18	
18-26		19-26	
27-30		27-30	

The older versions (English Revised and American Standard Bible) tend in general to have longer paragraphs, which, in the case of Chapter 1, coincide with the section divisions of the NIV. The more frequent paragraphs of the modern versions have, perhaps, more to do with readability and eye-appeal than they have to do with the accurate designation of the units of thought.

To avoid confusion, I will use the term **paragraph** (rather than section) which we could define as **a unit of thought** and which will normally consist of a main point along with a number of supporting points. The message or 'argument' of Philippians is carried by these units of thought, and as we follow them as they build on each other we will be enabled to see the flow of the argument, see where the author is taking us and begin to appreciate the role played by each separate paragraph.

THOUGHT-FLOW IN PHILIPPIANS 1

This is the moment we have been waiting for! Taking the text line by line and discovering in more detail what God wants to say to us.

Learning to identify the thought-flow is often the hardest element in Bible study. **It is also the most important**. So we need to take some time with this. Like learning to ride a bicycle it can be daunting at first. But once we learn it, we will have learned a skill that we will probably apply even without realising it every time we read the Bible.

As we do this, we will want to refer again and again to our map of contents which already indicates some of the movement of thought in this letter. We may wish to add things, to change things, so that we build a more accurate understanding of how the letter works.

So let's walk through Philippians Chapter 1 together.

IDENTIFYING THE PARAGRAPHS

There is broad agreement that in Philippians 1 there are **three paragraphs**. We can be reasonably confident then, that we will not go far wrong in following these three general divisions as we seek to investigate how this first part of Philippians fits together. At the same time, we should always keep open the possibility that the divisions provided by the NIV, or any other version, might ultimately not be the best, and before we are finished we might want to change them.

Paragraph 1: verses 1–2

> *Paul and Timothy, servants of Christ Jesus, to all the saints in Christ Jesus at Philippi, together with the overseers and deacons: Grace and peace to you from God our Father and the Lord Jesus Christ.*

It is easy to see what this paragraph is doing in the letter and what holds it together. It is the greeting. It also serves, as we have seen, to introduce some of the key issues in the letter, for it consists of greetings from servants of Christ to servants of Christ – the elders and deacons/servants.

Paul's desire is that the servants at Philippi will experience the grace and peace that only comes from God – we expect therefore that Paul will at some stage identify circumstances in which they particularly need such grace and peace.

The opening of the letter is not, therefore, simply a customary (and meaningless) greeting.

Paragraph 2: Verses 3–11.

> *I thank my God every time I remember you. In all my prayers for all of you, I always pray with joy because of your partnership in the gospel from the first day until now, being confident of this, that he who began a good work in you will carry it on to completion until the day of Christ Jesus. It is right for me to feel this way about all of you, since I have you in my heart; for whether I am in chains or defending and confirming the gospel, all of you share in God's grace with me. God can testify how I long for all of you with the affection of Christ Jesus. And this is my prayer: that your love may abound more and more in knowledge and depth of insight, so that you may be able to discern what is best and may be pure and blameless until the day of Christ, filled with the fruit of righteousness that comes through Jesus Christ — to the glory and praise of God.*

What binds this paragraph together is **prayer**. This is where it starts, and it ends with Paul setting out what it is he prays for them and why. So we can be fairly satisfied that verses 3-11 stand together as a paragraph or unit of thought. As a double check, the opening of verse 12 shows that Paul is moving on to a new issue, the question of how his seemingly negative circumstances have turned out to the advantage of the gospel.

Let's move closer and try to discern the building blocks of the paragraph, and as we do so it is often helpful to note certain words and phrases that carry the flow of thought, that link the various elements of the paragraph: words such as **'because of'**, **'since'**, **'for'**, **'so that'** – words that introduce explanation, or purpose.

For example, Paul's joy in his praying for them is linked to their partnership with him in his gospel work – **"because of your partnership..."** (1:3). Their involvement with him in turn appears to be linked to his conviction that God is really at work in their lives – that is, their commitment to the gospel is key evidence that they are believers. Paul's affection for them is thus totally justified, for they share with him in God's grace, and he can pray for them in the confidence that what God has started in them, he will complete.

Why do they need his prayers? God has clearly not finished with them yet, and for them to grow and develop even further Paul prays for them. This is, of course, evidence of Paul's love for them, evidence that Paul is a genuine servant.

And he goes on to spell out exactly what he prays for them. Why? Obviously because he wants them to know! Why does he want them to know? Because he wants them to be aware of what the spiritual goals are, and of what they need in order to achieve those spiritual goals. He prays specifically that their love will increase in knowledge and insight. We must conclude, in light of the focus on service, on spiritual work, that this perhaps unusual linking of love with knowledge and insight is exactly what servants of God need.

And what are the spiritual goals? Once again he spells them out: deepening discernment, purity of life, a life filled with the fruit of righteousness through Christ.

One other element that holds the paragraph together is the double reference to the **'day of Christ'**. This links God's work in them to their work and spiritual development for God. Both are set in the context of the day of Christ – the culmination of history. This gives the eternal dimension and therefore eternal urgency to both things: God's work in them, their work for God. It also demonstrates Paul's confidence in the salvation of the Philippians. And that is absolutely crucial to what he is about to call these folks to in the very next paragraph: to suffer just as he has suffered. How could you accept suffering with joy, how could you lay down your life for others through the gospel if there was no assurance that the gospel actually worked, and could actually bring folks right through to the eternal kingdom? It is because Paul is utterly confident that God will complete his work in them that he prays and works as he does.

THE BIG IDEA

It is always helpful to try to come up with a one sentence summary of what each paragraph is about. Otherwise we may content ourselves with too many loose ends and have only a very vague understanding of the core message. We might summarise this paragraph as follows:

> **Based on his confidence that God is at work in their lives and always carries through to completion what he starts, Paul, in his loving concern for them, prays for their spiritual growth and fruitfulness.**

We could call this the 'Big Idea' of the paragraph.

This is not by any means all that can be said about this paragraph, but it gives a clear understanding of the thought-flow and of the main focus. That in turn provides the context for us to engage in a more detailed study of the text and it shapes our understanding of how this passage can and should be applied to our own lives. We could make the Big Idea more prescriptive and applicational as follows:

> **In the confidence that God always finishes what he starts in people's lives, the onus is on us to commit to prayer for one another for spiritual growth and fruitfulness.**

Paragraph 3: Verses 12–30

> *Now I want you to know, brothers, that what has happened to me has really served to advance the gospel. As a result, it has become clear throughout the whole palace guard and to everyone else that I am in chains for Christ. Because of my chains, most of the brothers in the Lord have been encouraged to speak the word of God more courageously and fearlessly. It is true that some preach Christ out of envy and rivalry, but others out of goodwill. The latter do so in love, knowing that I am put here for the defence of the gospel. The former preach*

Christ out of selfish ambition, not sincerely, supposing that they can stir up trouble for me while I am in chains. But what does it matter? The important thing is that in every way, whether from false motives or true, Christ is preached. And because of this I rejoice. Yes, and I will continue to rejoice, for I know that through your prayers and the help given by the Spirit of Jesus Christ, what has happened to me will turn out for my deliverance. I eagerly expect and hope that I will in no way be ashamed, but will have sufficient courage so that now as always Christ will be exalted in my body, whether by life or by death. For to me, to live is Christ and to die is gain. If I am to go on living in the body, this will mean fruitful labour for me. Yet what shall I choose? I do not know! I am torn between the two: I desire to depart and be with Christ, which is better by far; but it is more necessary for you that I remain in the body. Convinced of this, I know that I will remain, and I will continue with all of you for your progress and joy in the faith, so that through my being with you again your joy in Christ Jesus will overflow on account of me. Whatever happens, conduct yourselves in a manner worthy of the gospel of Christ. Then, whether I come and see you or only hear about you in my absence, I will know that you stand firm in one spirit, contending as one man for the faith of the gospel without being frightened in any way by those who oppose you. This is a sign to them that they will be destroyed, but that you will be saved — and that by God. For it has been granted to you on behalf of Christ not only to believe on him, but also to suffer for him, since you are going through the same struggle you saw I had, and now hear that I still have.

This is a much longer paragraph. How do we know that it shouldn't really be two or three smaller paragraphs? Does it even matter?

Once again let's start by seeing if it holds together as a unit of thought. Can we find one key theme or a couple of very closely related themes that hold the paragraph together in such a way that it could not really be split up without doing damage to the thought-flow?

The first thing to note is that Paul has already referred to his **imprisonment** (verse 7). He now (verse 12) picks this up and in one way or another it is the issue of this entire paragraph.

Step 1: (12-13) he starts with the surprisingly positive impact of his imprisonment on his own work – the number of soldiers coming to faith.

Step 2: (14) he turns to its impact on Christian believers who up until his imprisonment had been reluctant to speak out for Christ, but who have now emerged from the shadows because of it.

Step 3: (15-21) he considers the impact on himself, complicated by the ulterior motives some have, seeking to cause Paul further difficulty. How will he react not just to persecution from opponents of the gospel but to injuries from his own side? Out of anger, selfishly losing sight of the gospel because of his personal hurts? That would cause great damage to the gospel. However, since for him living is Christ, he is prepared to take whatever he has to take, and with their prayerful support and the help of the Holy Spirit he is confident that he will escape this trap.

Step 4: (22-26) he considers the potential physical outcome: will this imprisonment lead to his death, or will he be released and therefore be able to return to them? Either way it will be gain for him, so there are no grounds for wallowing in self-pity.

Step 5: (27-30) finally, whatever the personal outcome, he urges them to stand fast together in the face of opposition, reminding them that it is part of their calling to suffer, just as he suffered when he first brought the gospel to Philippi (see Acts 16: 19-40) and as he is still suffering. Once again he relates this back to his confidence in their salvation: the fact that it has been granted to them to suffer is a sign, not that God has abandoned them, but that they have salvation!

Lots more could be said, but the five steps outlined cover the major movements Paul makes in this paragraph as he thinks through the issues raised by his imprisonment.

As we think about this paragraph, we may conclude that verses 27-30 should be treated as a paragraph on their own, for here Paul moves from a focus on his own situation, to a focus on theirs. That might help us to avoid confusing the two issues, although they are clearly related.

THE BIG IDEA

How should we summarise this paragraph, or these paragraphs? What is the **Big Idea**, for example, of verses 12-26?

Here is one suggestion:

> **Negative circumstances such as opposition, persecution, imprisonment and death, do not constitute an ultimate prison for the person for whom living is Christ and dying is gain, but rather an opportunity for the gospel.**

Take time **now** to do a similar exercise with Philippians Chapter 2. In doing so you might find the following check list useful.

PARAGRAPH STUDY GUIDE

1) Identify the **structure** of each paragraph with its **main statement(s)** and its **dependent statements** so that the flow of the argument will become clearer.
   a) Look out for linking words that serve to move the argument along: words like *therefore, so that, in order to, then.*
   b) Look for words which serve to support or illustrate the argument: *as, since, like, because, if.*

2) **The Big Idea:** try to identify the main point of the paragraph – the key statement or issue that holds it all together. Write a short sentence that summarises this main point (such as I have done for two paragraphs in Chapter 1).

3) Context: look carefully at what comes immediately before this paragraph, and what comes immediately after. How does this paragraph relate to this context? Is it

    a) basically a continuation?

    b) putting the other side, balancing what he has previously said?

    c) the start of a new main theme?

4) Wider context: how does this passage fit into the overall theme and purpose of Philippians?

5) Keep asking **'why' questions:** why is this passage important? Why does Paul say this at this particular point? Such 'why' questions help us to discern links, underlying issues and relevance.

6) Be careful to **include all the major elements:** this is where observation is so important – **actually seeing what is there**, and not what we think is there, or even what we would like to be there! Make sure you don't go chasing after your own hobby horses rather than following Paul's argument.

PHILIPPIANS CHAPTER 2 – THOUGHT FLOW

How did you get on?

One of the key themes of this entire chapter is that of attitude, or mindset. We can see the importance of this if we think of the big picture: the focus on God's work in us, and on our work together for God, particularly in seeking to spread the gospel – "contending as one man for the faith of the gospel" (1:27).

What God is seeking to produce in us and by definition, therefore, what we will need to work effectively together for him, is **the mind of Christ.**

So we could divide the chapter into 3 main paragraphs:

1. Paul's appeal to the Philippians to adopt the mind of Christ (1-18)
2. The mind of Christ as seen in Timothy (19-24)
3. The mind of Christ as seen in Epaphroditus (25-30)

This helps us to see at a glance the major movement of thought in this chapter. You may have decided, however, that verses 1–18 consist of a number of separate yet connected parts:

- 1-5 focus on Paul's appeal to them to harmony and an unselfish regard for others

- 6–11 give us the key to this and the chief example: the mindset of Christ and the key attitude of humble self-sacrifice in obedience to the Father

- 12-18 spell out the appropriate response to this as Paul appeals to them to live obediently as God's children in a perverse world, just as Jesus did, not characterised by the selfish complaining and grumbling that characterises the world, following also Paul's example, who is prepared to pour himself out for them, living in the light of the coming reality of the 'day of Christ'

Once again, there is so much more that could be said, but at least we have set out the main flow of thought and how this part of the letter relates to the whole. It remains for you to work through the final two chapters for yourself!

THE ART OF OBSERVATION

In a really good detective story all the clues are given to the reader as well as to the detective. In that sense we all see the same thing. However, there is a difference between **seeing** and **noticing**. Where the detective proves his or her worth is in noticing what others do not.

The art of observation – of seeing what is really there – is a difficult art. It takes practice and patience. And it is critical to the whole process of Bible reading and study. I have been present in many Bible studies where people have commented on things that are **not** in the text.

Here is a delightful story that illustrates the point better than anything I have ever read:

The Student, the Fish and Agassiz[1] – by the Student[2]

It was more than fifteen years ago that I entered the laboratory of Professor Agassiz , and told him I had enrolled my name in the scientific school as a student of natural history. He asked me a few questions about my object in coming, the mode in which I afterwards proposed to use the knowledge I might acquire and finally, whether I wished to study any special branch. To the latter I replied that while I wished to be well grounded in all departments of zoology, I purposed to devote myself specially to insects.

"When do you wish to begin?" he asked.

"Now," I replied.

This seemed to please him, and with an energetic "very well," he reached from a shelf a huge jar of specimens in yellow alcohol.

"Take this fish," said he, "and look at it; we call it a Haemulon; by and by I will ask what you have seen."

With that he left me. In ten minutes I had seen all that could be seen in that

[1] Louis Agassiz (1807-1873) was a renowned Swiss scientist and teacher, famous for his work on the fossil records of fish and on glaciation, who became a professor at Harvard (Boston, USA) and had a major influence on the development of science in North America.

[2] After this account was published anonymously, the 'student' was identified as Samuel H Scudder.

fish, and started in search of the professor, who had, however, left the museum; and when I returned, after lingering over some of the odd animals stored in the upper apartment, my specimen was dried all over. I dashed the fluid over the fish as if to resuscitate it from a fainting-fit, and looked with anxiety for a return of a normal, sloppy appearance. This little excitement over, nothing was to be done but return to a steadfast gaze at my mute companion. Half an hour passed, an hour, another hour; the fish began to look loathsome. I turned it over and around; looked it in the face – ghastly; from behind, beneath, above, sideways, at a three-quarters view – just as ghastly. I was in despair; at an early hour I concluded that lunch was necessary; so with infinite relief, the fish was carefully replaced in the jar, and for an hour I was free.

On my return, I learned that Professor Agassiz had been at the museum, but had gone and would not return for several hours. Slowly I drew forth that hideous fish, and with a feeling of desperation again looked at it. I might not use a magnifying glass; instruments of all kinds were interdicted. My two hands, my two eyes, and the fish; it seemed a most limited field. I began to count the scales in the different rows until I was convinced that was nonsense. At last a happy thought struck me – I would draw the fish; and now with surprise I began to discover new features in the creature. Just then the professor returned.

"That is right," said he, "a pencil is one of the best eyes. I am glad to notice, too, that you keep your specimen wet and your bottle corked."

With these encouraging words he added, "Well, what is it like?"

He listened attentively to my brief rehearsal of the structure of parts whose names were still unknown to me: fringed gill-arches, fleshly lips, lidless eyes; the lateral line, the spinous fin, and the forked tail. When I had finished, he waited as if expecting more, and then, with an air of disappointment:

"You have not looked very carefully. Why," he continued, more earnestly, "you haven't seen one of the most conspicuous features of the animal, which is as plainly before your eyes as the fish itself. Look again; look again!" and he left me to my misery.

I was mortified. Still more of that wretched fish? But now I set myself to the task with a will, and discovered one new thing after another, until I saw how just the professor's criticism had been. The afternoon passed quickly, and when towards its close, the professor inquired, "Do you see it yet?"

"No," I replied. "I am certain I do not, but see how little I saw before."

"That is next best," said he earnestly, "but I won't hear you now; put away your fish and go home; perhaps you will be ready with a better answer in the morning. I will examine you before you look at the fish."

This was disconcerting; not only must I think of the fish all night, studying without the object before me, what this unknown but most visible feature might be, but also, without reviewing my new discoveries, I must give an exact account of them the next day.

The cordial greeting from the professor the next morning was reassuring; here was a man who seemed to be quite as anxious as I that I should see for myself what he saw.

"Do you perhaps mean," I asked, "that the fish has symmetrical sides with paired organs?"

His thoroughly pleased, "Of course, of course!" repaid the wakeful hours of the previous night. After he had discoursed most happily and enthusiastically – as he always did on the importance of this point – I ventured to ask what I should do next.

"Oh, look at your fish!" he said, and left me again to my own devices. In a little more than an hour he returned and heard my new catalogue.

"That is good, that is good!" he repeated, "but that is not all; go on." And for three long days, he placed that fish before my eyes, forbidding me to look at anything else, or to use any artificial aid. "Look, look, look," was his repeated injunction.

This was the best entomological lesson I ever had – a lesson whose influence has extended to the details of every subsequent study; a legacy the professor has left to me, as he left it to many others, of inestimable value, which we could not buy, with which we cannot part. [15]

Look, look, look! This cannot be stressed enough. We need to discipline ourselves and train ourselves to notice what is there.

[3] Published in American Poems, 3rd Ed, Houghton, Osgood & Co, 1879, pp450-454

WHAT WE NEED TO NOTICE

Although we have already encountered some of them, it might be helpful at this stage to set out a more detailed list of **the basic building blocks** of sentences and paragraphs so that we have a better idea of what to look for, what to notice.

- **Pronouns** – words such as 'I', 'we', 'you', 'they'. Always ask: who are the 'they', who is the 'I'? Note that the English pronoun 'you' can be either singular or plural. Most often in the New Testament it is used in the plural – the exhortations are mostly written to people in community (something which we in the West, with our individualistic approach to life might miss!).

- **Verbs** – these are the words that express the action. Note in particular the tense of the verb: is it present, or past, or future? Is it active (he killed) or passive (he was killed)?

- **Key 'clauses' that carry the argument**

  * Conditional clauses – often these have an 'if... then' framework, although in English the 'then' tends to be omitted.

  * Purpose clauses – where there is an implied 'in order that/to...'

  * Result clauses – where there is an implied 'so that/with the result that'.

- **Conjunctions** – words that connect parts of a sentence, such as 'but', 'and', 'for' and which also carry the flow of thought.

- **Metaphor/figures of speech** – where words are used in a sense other than the literal sense. This can come in the form of a noun: "God gave us a **door** for the gospel"; it is also often carried by a verb: "a land **flowing** with milk and honey".

- **Questions** – sometimes a writer will use a rhetorical question and then proceed to answer it.

- **Lists** – if a writer gives lists of qualities, for example, consider if and how they are grouped together.

- **Contrasts and comparisons** – one of the most effective ways of communicating truth is by means of comparison and contrast.

- **Repetition** – key words and ideas are often repeated throughout a book.

- **Balance** – watch out for this feature where an author will first present one aspect of an issue, and then a balancing aspect.

- **Tone** – pay attention to the author's tone: is it critical, encouraging, hopeful, emotive, pleading, angry?

And now an exercise in noticing. There follows a passage from Philippians 4. Take time over it, read it, re-read it and read it again. As you read **jot down your observations**, either in a list following the text (or in your notebook) or in the text itself. It might be helpful to copy out the text, either longhand or on your word processor, leaving plenty of space between the lines in which to make your observations. Or you could photocopy the passage as it is set out here and write on that.

Use the above list to guide you at first if this exercise is very new. Turn the headings into questions: are there any examples of repetition? Any lists? To whom do the pronouns refer? Is there any use of metaphor? Any conditional/purpose/result clauses? Any emotive language? What is the tone of the passage? Does it change? What are the key verbs? What tenses are used?

You will not find examples of everything in this passage, but many items on our check list are illustrated.

When will you know when you are finished? I'm not suggesting "three long days"! But perhaps you should try to note down **at least fifty** observations. **Look, look, look!**

I plead with Euodia and I plead with Syntyche to agree with each other

in the Lord. Yes, and I ask you, loyal yokefellow, help these women who

have contended at my side in the cause of the gospel, along with

Clement and the rest of my fellow workers, whose names are in the book of life.

Rejoice in the Lord always. I will say it again: Rejoice! Let your

gentleness be evident to all. The Lord is near. Do not be anxious about

anything, but in everything, by prayer and petition, with thanksgiving,

present your requests to God. And the peace of God, which transcends

all understanding, will guard your hearts and your minds in Christ Jesus.

What did you notice?

Here are some basic observations to give an idea of the kinds of things that could/should be noted at this stage:

- Names and pronouns
  * addresses the folks in dispute by name - how would they have felt to hear their names read out?
  * asks a third party to help – a personal request
  * two women
  * women who have been engaged in gospel work
  * they have been Paul's associates
  * on a team with Clement and other fellow workers
  * names in the book of life (cf Luke 10:20)

- Tone
  * pleading, strong appeal to them to sort themselves out
  * positive: rejoice
  * not angry or bullish

- Repetition
  * rejoice x 2
  * in the Lord, in Christ Jesus

- List
  * prayer, petition, thanksgiving, present requests

- Result clause
  * and the peace of God, etc

- Key verbs
  * agree with each other
  * help
  * present your requests

- Metaphor
  * guard hearts and minds

- Commands
  * rejoice
  * do not be anxious

- Key conjunctions
  * But

- Balance
  * negative 'do not be anxious about anything' with positive '**but** present your requests'
  * 'anything' with 'everything'

- Contrast
  * 'anxiety' with 'peace'
  * 'being anxious' with 'presenting requests'

A MATTER OF INTERPRETATION

When it comes to the question of interpreting what the Bible says it is possible for unhealthy concern, approaching panic, to set in. To be sure, misunderstandings happen all the time in our verbal communications with each other, but the fact is that most of us use a great many words every day, we assume that real communication and understanding takes place, and most of the time we are right! Don't underestimate your ability to grasp the plain, straightforward sense of what God is saying. God's desire is to communicate his truth with us. Not only has he given us his words, he has also given us his Holy Spirit to guide and teach us.

At the same time, the Bible is not written at the level of a children's story book or the local newspaper. It is God's Word. As God reveals his character, his thinking, his purposes we must expect a depth of meaning that ultimately goes beyond our finite human ability to grasp fully this side of heaven. That doesn't mean that we can grasp nothing. It simply means that however much we understand, there will always be more to be understood.

In addition, some of the language and argumentation of the Bible is complex. With disarming honesty Peter tells us that some of Paul's writings "contain some things that are hard to understand, which ignorant and unstable people distort, as they do the other scriptures, to their own destruction" (2 Peter 3:16). He goes on to warn us not to be carried away by such error, but rather to grow in the grace and knowledge of our Lord Jesus Christ.

The warning is necessary, not just because of the danger of false teaching by the 'ignorant and unstable', but also because sincere and devoted believers in Christ can come unstuck over biblical interpretation. Many of us will already have had the experience of sitting in on a Bible discussion and hearing different people expressing not only different but contradictory views on a part of Scripture without any final resolution being arrived at, and, more frequently these days, without any final resolution being sought!

Increasingly people appear happy to exist with contradiction, particularly in the West, where a whole generation has now grown up suspicious of any authority, of any definitive meaning, believing that truth means different things to different people. This inevitably leads to a situation where anyone's opinion (or guess) is as good as anyone else's. And it means that any objective understanding of truth - as something which is absolutely true for all people at all time, whether they believe it or not – is ultimately impossible. Even those of us who still believe in objective truth can be influenced more than we think by the prevailing pressures of relativism and tolerance of mutually contradictory viewpoints.

D A Carson tells this interesting story:

> *About twenty years ago I rode in a car with a fellow believer who relayed to me what the Lord had 'told' him that morning in his quiet time. He had been reading the KJV [King James'Version of the Bible] of Matthew; and I perceived that not only had he misunderstood the archaic English, but also that the KJV had unwittingly misrepresented the Greek text. I gently suggested there might be another way to understand the passage and summarised what I thought the passage was saying. The brother dismissed my view as impossible on the grounds that the Holy Spirit, who does not lie, had told him the truth on this matter. Being young and bold, I pressed on with my explanation of grammar, context, and translation, but was brushed off by a reference to 1 Corinthians 2:10b-15: spiritual things must be spiritually discerned – which left little doubt about my status. Genuinely intrigued, I asked this brother what he would say if I put forward my interpretation, not on the basis of grammar and text, but on the basis that the Lord himself had given me the interpretation I was advancing. He was silent a long time, and then concluded, 'I guess that would mean the Spirit says the Bible means different things to different people.'* [1]

[1] D A Carson, Exegetical Fallacies 2nd Ed, Baker, 1996, pp 16,17, Footnote 2

His story raises a number of different issues, but the key one in our context is that when we find two contradictory and mutually incompatible statements of the **meaning** of a particular Bible passage, **both of them cannot be right!** And we must not lay the blame for such contradictory views at the door of the Holy Spirit.

We need, therefore, to be careful in our interpretation of Scripture that we do not shift our approach from 'what the Bible means' to 'what the Bible means to me', as opposed to what it means to someone else. Bible truth is objective truth: justification by faith carries the same objective reality in Belfast as it does in Buenos Aires: Irishmen and Argentinians are justified on exactly the same grounds!

It is true that there are frequently what we might call **different levels of meaning** in a passage, where these levels are not at all contradictory but rather **build upon** and **complement** each other. But if we believe both in objective truth and in the Holy Spirit, the Spirit of truth, we cannot subscribe to the view that the same Bible text can mean different things in the sense of mutually contradictory things.

The **application** of biblical truth is another matter. Let's not confuse meaning with application. When it comes to **application** the same biblical truth may be applied in a host of different contexts and in a host of different cultures. So while discrimination on grounds of wealth is as much sin in India as it is in Canada, how such discrimination manifests itself may vary greatly between the two cultures; the application a Canadian might immediately see in the text might never occur to an Indian, and vice versa.

Our first concern, then, must be with what a given text means, and only then with how the spiritual truth it contains applies in the corporate or individual situation in which we find ourselves. The challenge Paul gives us through his words to Timothy is that we become those who correctly handle the word of truth (2 Timothy 2:15).

With Peter's warning and Paul's challenge in mind, let's return to where we started this unit. All of us use language everyday in the expectation that 9 times out of 10 we can both make ourselves understood and understand what is said to us. Consider the following:

"Sarah went into town by bus today and bought £10 worth of food."

Someone unfamiliar with our setting might ask which town Sarah went into. A person from another country might need to know what £10 is in their currency. Someone else might want to know what a bus is. Going deeper, someone might want to know exactly what food Sarah bought, why Sarah had to go into town, why the bus instead of a car, and why Sarah didn't spend the money on something else. There is plenty to explain and explore, and some meaning which we will never know unless the speaker gives us the additional information. But **the main message is clear.**

Could we interpret the statement to mean "I stayed at home today and watched a TV programme about cooking"? Surely not! The main message is clear.

If we approach the Bible this way we will find that its main message is clear and understandable. In Philippians, for example, Paul makes the following statement about the Lord Jesus:

> God exalted him to the highest place and gave him the name that is above every name, that at the name of Jesus every knee should bow, in heaven and on earth and under the earth, and every tongue confess that Jesus Christ is Lord..." (Philippians 2:9-11)

Some of the statements here go beyond our ability to grasp. How can we fully appreciate, for example, what is the 'highest place'? In addition, we might want to know what the phrase 'under the earth' means or when it is that this acknowledgement of Jesus will take place. But could we understand Paul to mean, "Jesus is just one of a number of equally great people", or "Jesus lived, died and that was the end of him"? Of course not. We may not understand every phrase, but it would not be correct to say that the main message is unclear and that we cannot be confident that we understand it.

Now, let's have a little fun!

AWKWARD ALEC (OR ALICE)

During a recent Bible study at **Anytown Evangelical Church** the enthusiastic group found their efforts to grapple with the text of Philippians frequently sabotaged by the deadly duo of Alec and Alice (unrelated except by approach to the Bible) who came up with the following 'interpretations' and 'applications' (which, they were sure, were given to them by the Holy Spirit himself).

A. 1:4 "I always pray with joy" – the true applications of this statement are a) I only pray when I feel good; b) all prayer should be full of joy and there is no place for a sad prayer or for intercessory prayer.

B. 1:12 Paul tells us that his imprisonment has "really served to advance the gospel." We, therefore, should seek to be imprisoned in order that the gospel might advance.

C. 1:18 "But what does it matter? The important thing is that in every way, whether from false motives or true, Christ is preached. And because of this I rejoice." Paul is teaching that the motives of a preacher are of no importance. The person who preaches from selfish ambition is quite acceptable (indeed Paul encourages it).

D. 1:23 "I am torn between the two: I desire to depart and be with Christ, which is better by far; but it is more necessary for you that I remain in the body." This suggests that Paul was suicidal when he wrote this letter because he did not know whether to choose to live or die.

E. 1:27 "...contending as one man for the faith of the gospel..." The important task of 'contending for the faith' is open to men only.

F. 2:3 "Do nothing out of selfish ambition or vain conceit, but in humility consider others better than yourselves." Alec believes he is entitled to sit back and do little in church because everyone else is better than he is. Although Alice is a qualified piano teacher, she will not play the piano in church but gives way to a novice musician because she is required to consider others to be better than herself.

G. 2:14 "Do everything without complaining or arguing." Since Christians are told never to complain, they should never complain, for example, about the food or service in a restaurant. Since Christians are told never to argue, a) they should not become lawyers; b) they should not seek to discuss or debate their faith with unbelievers in case it descends into 'argument'.

H. 4:13 "I can do everything through him who gives me strength." Through God's power Christians can do anything they want. If it does not work out in practice it is through lack of faith on their part.

Do you agree with their interpretations and the applications where suggested? If not (and I don't!) how would you have answered them? Do any general principles emerge that will help to guard us against the sort of mistakes Alec and Alice are making?

THE IMPORTANCE OF CONTEXT

In some cases the awkward interpretations arise from a simple misreading of the words. In most cases the true interpretation can be found through examining not only the meaning of the individual words, but from seeing **how they are used in their immediate context.** (Context literally means 'what goes with the text'.) In some cases we can additionally appeal to the larger context of the book.

In example **F**, considering others better than ourselves has nothing to do with whether they do things better than we do, but rather it has to do with how we value them as persons. Alec and Alice have misinterpreted the language used.

They have made the same mistake with example **E**, interpreting the word 'man' as meaning male as opposed to female. The word can, of course, be used in that way, but not here. The word 'man' is part of an English idiom – to do something as one man – which expresses unity and solidarity and togetherness. It is how the NIV has chosen to translate the word 'psyche = soul', so in actual fact no idea of male as opposed to female is in the original language. (The word 'man' is increasingly seen these days as referring to man as male, and therefore the word 'person' might be a wiser choice for the translators to avoid negative reaction from a modern audience!)

In most cases context will come to our help. In the first example Paul's joy is in direct relation to their partnership with him in the gospel and has nothing to do with some unrelated joyful state in which he must be in order to pray.

Example C is more complex but again can be answered by its context. Paul's point is **not** that all motivation is equally valid and acceptable. His point is rather that despite the mixture of motives, Christ is being presented and this is what he rejoices in. His focus on Chapter 1 is to demonstrate how God is at work despite difficult circumstances of all kinds. He makes it clear at the start of Chapter 2 and again in Chapter 3 that having the correct motivation in our service is of critical importance, but that is not his focus in Chapter 1.

This helps illustrate another general point: we need to be careful not to make every statement in the Bible apply absolutely in every situation.

The final example is another illustration of this point. Even though Paul uses the word **"everything"**, he means everything in a particular context. Paul is not a superman – leaping tall buildings, catching bullets in his hand and out-flying jet planes! In context Paul is talking about coping with material resources and their absence. Sometimes he has plenty; sometimes he is in great material need. Whatever his circumstances he has discovered the secret of contentment: he can cope with everything because of the strength God supplies. It is of course true to say that God gives us the strength to do what he calls us to do, but that is not the point Paul is making in Philippians 4.

We must train ourselves, then, constantly to **consider every statement in the light of its immediate context**, and in the light of the wider context of the chapter and book in which it is found. There is more to interpretation than simply understanding the words that are used. We are looking for the significance of the words.

THE IMPACT OF CONTEXT ON SIGNIFICANCE

Let's return to the statement used earlier in this unit: **"Sarah went into town by bus today and bought £10 worth of food."** This statement makes perfectly good sense by itself. We do not need to know the wider context to understand the meaning either of the individual words or of the sentence in which they occur. However, if we want to know the **significance of the statement** – why it was said, why it matters – we will need to know the context.

Consider the following scenarios.

> **A.** Sarah has been ill for many weeks. For a while it was touch and go as to whether she would live. But there has been a recent, dramatic improvement. So the statement that she went into town and did some shopping illustrates just how much her health has improved.

> **B.** Sarah is one of five people each of whom won a £10 prize at a recent event. All the others had already spent their money, but Sarah kept hers until today. In this context the statement focuses on the fact that a) she has now spent her money, and b) she spent it on food.

> **C.** Sarah bought a car two years ago and drove it a great deal before she had an accident. In this context our statement indicates that she still lacks the confidence to drive her car into town.

Each context adds significance to the basic meaning of the statement. Or to put this another way: knowing the context helps us to see the point of the statement: not simply to understand the words, but to get the message.

This will help us to understand why it is that in the Gospels we sometimes find the same incident recorded in two or more accounts, set in a different context in each. For example, Luke and Mark both record the incident of the healing of the blind beggar, Bartimaeus, at Jericho.[2] Luke puts it in the context of a discussion between Christ and the people, of the difficulty of the rich in entering the kingdom of God. Mark puts his account in the context of the request made by James and John to sit in the prime seats in the kingdom. How are we to understand this difference?

It is not that one of the writers has got things wrong, or, even worse, has falsified the historical records. All of these incidents happened – they are historically true. Nor are the writers contradicting each other. As with Sarah's story, the different contexts serve to bring out the different significances or messages carried by the same event.

In the example mentioned, Mark surely wants us to contrast Christ's words to the beggar, **'What do you want me to do for you?'** with the self-serving ambition of his disciples. Luke on the other hand wants to illustrate both in this story and the next (the story of Zacchaeus) the fact that it is possible for both the poor and the rich to be saved. Both authors are being guided by the Holy Spirit to bring out a different aspect of the same incident.

Note that in the above example concerning Sarah not only are all three meanings possible, depending on context, but **they are not mutually exclusive:** all three could be true at the same time.

[2] Mark 10:46-52; Luke 18:35-43

We have already seen how important the wider context of the passage is in understanding the significance of Paul's often quoted statement, **'I can do everything through him who gives me strength.'** As a brief exercise, consider the following statements in their context in Philippians, asking ourselves not just what the words mean but what is the point of each statement in its context:

A. 1:21 **"For to me, to live is Christ and to die is gain."**

B. 2:7 **"...but made himself nothing, taking the very nature of a servant..."**

C. 4:9 **"The God of peace..."**

MORE ABOUT CONTEXT

So far we have considered the paramount importance of the immediate context of the passage in understanding any statement of Scripture. Context is broader than this. In the opening Units of this guide we spent a great deal of time considering the big picture of Philippians so that we could read the significance of each individual paragraph against the background of the overall purpose of the book.

We have also briefly considered the theological context of the Bible as a whole and the importance of ensuring that we control our interpretation of individual statements by keeping in mind the overall teaching of the Bible.

In addition to that we often will need to consider the historical and cultural context in which and into which the Bible books were written. A primary principle of Biblical interpretation is first to **understand what a statement meant to its original audience.**

Philippians is so called because it was written to a particular group of believers in a particular geographical location at a particular time in history. This of course does not mean that the book is irrelevant to us. Philippians is part of God's writing, God's Word for all believers, both at the time it was written and at all times since – in this sense it transcends time. It does mean, however, that Philippians was read, studied and (hopefully) applied in Philippi in the 1st Century. It must have made sense to them.

Quite a distance separates us from them – historically, geographically and culturally. It is important that we try to identify where this distance actually lies and be careful not to exaggerate it, for while cultures change radically from country to country and age to age, human beings at heart remain remarkably similar. The human heart is sick in all cultures, and the spiritual diseases are fundamentally very much the same.

Again this is often an issue of common sense and should cause us no panic, but it is useful to keep it in mind. For example, Philippians tells us that Paul is in prison as he writes. It might be helpful, particularly for those of us in certain Western societies, to try to gain an accurate picture of what prison in Paul's day would have been like and not to confuse it in our thinking with the more humane and technologically sophisticated surroundings in which prisoners are detained in some parts of the world today.

At various points in Philippians we will find that a basic knowledge of local conditions in terms of health care, the economy and education can be helpful. At other points, particularly in Chapter 3, the religious context, and particularly that of Judaistic influences, is important.

Where can such background information be found? A good Bible dictionary and/or encyclopaedia will provide a great deal of useful information. An excellent resource is the *IVP Bible Background Commentary: New Testament,* by Craig Keener (IVP, 1993). A more detailed commentary on Philippians such as that by Gordon Fee[3] will also provide much help here, both in its introduction and scattered throughout the text. In addition, we also have the information in Acts 16 as to how the church at Philippi was formed. (Interestingly we will discover there that what happened in a prison had a great deal to do with it!)

If you have access to a Bible dictionary, a commentary or other background resources it would be a good thing to use it now and to try to find out information relevant to our understanding of Philippians:

A. **The city of Philippi** – location, population, prestige and reputation in the second half of the1st Century

B. **Economic conditions**

C. **Infrastructure** – travel, health care, education, local government and institutions

D. **Religion** – religious pluralism and religious/philosophical worldviews. (This can be particularly helpful. Note how Paul in 2:15 refers to the society of the time as a "crooked and depraved generation". In what ways were they depraved and crooked? Is there any background information which might help us understand what he is referring to here? Note also in Chapter 3 where Paul warns them about "those dogs, those men who do evil, those mutilators of the flesh" – who were they? What background might be helpful to us here?

E. **Culture** – are there any statements in Philippians which reveal attitudes, values, customs which are particular to the culture of the day and about which we must be careful in our application? For example, in 2 Corinthians 13:12 Paul tells the believers to greet one another with a holy kiss. Do we need to distinguish between the underlying principle (the importance of greeting one another and keeping our greetings holy) and the custom (kissing one another is not culturally acceptable amongst acquaintances in certain Western countries at least)?

[3] Paul's Letter to the Philippians, The New International Commentary on the New Testament, Eerdmans Publishing Co, 1995

MORE ABOUT CULTURE

This last point is particularly important and needs a little more consideration. How can we tell what is culturally conditioned? Do all the commands of the New Testament apply to us or can some of them be legitimately set aside as belonging only to the culture of their day?

Let's consider two issues which are mentioned in the New Testament:

- the practice of eating meat offered to idols
- the practice of washing one another's feet.

Judging by the amount of space devoted to it, the question of whether Christians should eat meat that had been offered to idols was a major issue in the early church. It occupies a considerable section of 1 Corinthians – Chapters 8 to 10. Now I have to say that I have never faced this precise issue myself in my cultural context. Does that mean that three chapters of the New Testament are largely irrelevant to me? Not at all. While I may never face the specific issue, the underlying principles taught by Paul in these chapters have wide application: the principle, for example, of not causing a brother or sister to stumble in their faith through my insistence on exercising my personal rights and freedoms; the principle that food will not commend us to God – we are neither the worse spiritually if we do not eat, nor the better if we do eat.

What about **washing one another's feet?** This was clearly a custom in society at the time (see John 13) – or at least it was customary for a servant to do it. Yet there are very few churches in the West that practise this custom. Why is that? It is not simply for reasons of cultural difference that we don't do this in most Christian communities that I know. The fact is that its context in John 13, and the teaching drawn from it by the Lord himself, make it clear that **Christ intended his disciples to understand it metaphorically and spiritually.** It was an enacted parable. We are to do to others as we have allowed Christ to do to us. To allow him to wash our feet means to allow him to serve us by cleansing and sanctifying our life and character. As we allow him to do that to us, so we are to do that to our brothers and sisters: giving ourselves up for them in such a way as to help produce holy, more beautiful people (see Ephesians 5:25-28).

There is no evidence that the command in John 13 to wash one another's feet had the literal force and application of, for example, the command to be baptised, or to remember Christ through taking bread and wine together. Both the context and the rest of the New Testament make this clear.

In the end, very few of the commands of the New Testament[4] could legitimately be said to be culturally relative and we must be careful not to be found using culture as an excuse to reject teaching which goes against the grain of our own prevailing cultural beliefs and practices. Just because, for example, consumerism characterises much of Western culture does not mean that Christians should be characterised by it within those cultures, any more than the existence of polygamy in certain cultures can be made to justify Christians having multiple spouses.

Today's world throws up all kinds of challenges in this area. As we face these challenges in our interpretation of the Bible it might be helpful to remember the following:

[4] This is not the case for Old Testament commands. Principles that will help us correctly interpret and apply the Old Testament can be found in Chapters 13 and 14.

- No culture comes to us untainted by sin. All culture must therefore be brought under the critique of Biblical teaching and principles. The gospel challenges all cultures, especially our own.

- Our first concern must be to seek to understand what the New Testament is saying clearly on a given subject, then to see if any of this can be set aside on the grounds of being applicable only to the culture of its day.

- Much less of the New Testament is culturally relative than we might at first imagine.

- Specific applications to 1st Century culture will contain principles which we must apply to our own cultural situation. If we decide, for example, that the covering or uncovering of heads (1 Corinthians 11) is no longer a helpful or necessary symbol in today's church (and on this sincere Christians differ) we are surely not at liberty to set aside the underlying principles of headship.

OLD TESTAMENT BACKGROUND TO THE NEW

The New Testament did not come to us in isolation, rather as the final stage of the written revelation of God to us. We should expect, then, that every New Testament book will contain references and allusions to the Old Testament, some of which will be more obvious than others. One of the benefits of having a Bible which provides references in the margin of the page, or as footnotes, is that these will highlight the more obvious Old Testament quotations or allusions whenever they occur.

At first sight Philippians appears to be the exception! The NIV study Bible tells us that Philippians contains no Old Testament quotations. This is true in the sense that there are no explicit citations, but it is not the whole story.

A number of the key issues raised in Philippians require an understanding of Old Testament teaching and background. This is particularly the case in Chapter 3 where Paul refers to believers in Christ as being **the circumcision** and where he refers to his own background in Judaism. An understanding of the purposes and symbolism of circumcision will be central to our interpretation of Paul's teaching in this chapter, and there is considerable Old Testament material on this, as we would expect.

A second issue of importance in Philippians which has its background in the Old Testament is that of sacrifice. Paul specifically refers to this on two occasions. In 2:17 he states "But even if I am being poured out like a drink offering on the sacrifice and service coming from your faith, I am glad and rejoice with all of you." And again in 4:18 he refers to their financial gift as 'a fragrant offering, an acceptable sacrifice, pleasing to God.' The background of Leviticus is strong here and it raises the issue of the 'priesthood' of believers: what constitutes an acceptable sacrifice? What kind of sacrifices are we to offer?

Those who wish to take these matters further might note that Philippians 4 also deals with the question of 'peace' and its enjoyment, and that one entire offering in the Old Testament system was to do with peace (called the 'fellowship offering' by the NIV). It is just possible that what God was teaching his people in symbolic form in Leviticus 3, about how they might have and enjoy peace and fellowship both with him and with each other, might have some connection with what Paul is teaching here.

PERSONAL CONTEXT

Before leaving this unit it might be useful to be reminded that in addition to the various contexts we have discussed – immediate, whole book, historical, cultural, Old Testament – we bring **ourselves** to the text.

None of us comes empty-handed or empty-headed to our shared task of studying the Bible. Each of us comes pre-shaped by our religious background (if any), our upbringing, our cultural surroundings, our experiences and personality. We all already have a world-view – a way of seeing the world around us. Our world-view is more or less biblical depending on the influences that have impacted us to this point.

To ground this personally, for a moment: I am Scots-Irish, born and bred in Northern Ireland, from a Brethren background and a middle-class family. (Some might be tempted to say at this point that I might as well give up any hope of understanding the Bible with that set of influences!) I am also apparently, in terms of my temperament, an 'ENFP' – more extrovert than introvert, more intuitive than cognitive, more at home with poetry than history, art than science, words than numbers, pictures than concepts. All of this will impact my approach.

One of our key purposes in coming to the Bible is that, rather than sit in judgement on it in accordance with our already formed way of understanding reality, we allow it to sit in judgement on us. We do not come to Scripture to create meaning, we come to find meaning. In short, we come to Scripture to be changed.

"Do not conform any longer to the pattern of this world" Paul exhorts us, *"but be transformed by the renewing of your mind." (Romans 12:2)*

Some of the unhelpful baggage we bring with us to the Bible – and remember that not all baggage is unhelpful – is easy to spot. Some is deeply ingrained: difficult to see and even more difficult to remove. But it is good to become increasingly aware of it. (Just turned fifty, I am still discovering new things about myself in this area!)

It is perhaps easy to see, for example, that strongly negative experiences with our own father can cloud our appreciation of God as Father. We may need help to untangle this in our lives. In addition, some of the damage we have done to ourselves through pride and selfishness can prevent us from seeing ourselves as God sees us and therefore deeply hinder the process of recognition, repentance and co-operation with the activity of God's Spirit in our lives.

Matters are complicated further by the increasing domination of feelings, experience, desires and expectations of material comfort and happiness in contemporary Western culture. Without realising it we can allow these things to shape the glasses through which we see Scripture, in much the same way as others may come to the Bible with a pre-formed theological system which they impose on the text.

All of us run the risk of using Scripture for our own purposes. So from time to time it is good to take our glasses off, examine them, give them a good clean, and perhaps even have an eye test to see if we need new lenses!

And here we can be greatly helped and enriched by studying the Scriptures with others. I have friends from a wide range of cultural and religious backgrounds. Steve, brought up as a child in Korea and as a teenager and adult in the US, will have different perspectives than will Timothy, brought up in rural Tanzania with some years of education in Kenya. Interacting together we can help point out some of the cultural or personal blind spots that each of us may have.

THE POWER OF WORDS

However wonderful and complex they are, animals are rather limited in their communication. When a lion wishes to compliment a lioness or to tell her of his love, his options are few! Not so with us humans. And while there can be significant wordless communication, there is no doubting the advantage of human language when it comes to expressing ourselves.

Words are wonderful things – like musical notes they can be woven together in a seemingly infinite variety of patterns to convey meaning. They have immense power, to hurt and to heal, to provoke and to calm, to bring together and to split apart. A few words are all it takes to plunge nations into war, to pronounce that the tests are clear, to reveal treachery, to set in motion the best and worst of times.

To read and study the Bible is, by definition, to engage in an endless love-affair with words. While the Bible is more than words on pages, it is not less.

In this chapter and the next I want to focus briefly on two further aspects of this intense engagement with words which we have to date largely ignored:

- the power of figurative language
- the benefits (as well as some of the pitfalls) of word studies

THE POWER OF FIGURATIVE LANGUAGE

The very mention of figurative language is likely to cause some to cough nervously and clutch at their throats (figuratively speaking of course!). But it need not. We all use figurative language much more than we realise and still generally manage to understand one another perfectly well. Rather than being a barrier to communication it enhances it, and lends to language a richness that all can enjoy.

Remember all those wonderful words from language class: metaphor, simile, symbol, image. These are often classed together under the general heading of **metaphor**. Now, the dictionary definition of metaphor is rather dull: *a figure of speech in which a word or phrase is applied to an object or action that it does not literally apply to in order to imply a resemblance.*[1] Robertson McQuilkin defines figurative language like this: *words that are used with a meaning other than their common, literal sense.*[2]

Examples are much easier to understand. *She has an appetite for her work. He is a lion in defence.* We take a word or concept from one area of experience and transfer it to another where it communicates on a figurative rather than on a literal level. In these examples, the concept of physical hunger has been transferred to the arena of work, while the qualities associated with a literal lion (at least some of them!) have been transferred to the arena of sport. The statements are not 'literally' true: they are not claiming that the woman is experiencing literal hunger pangs, nor that the man has claws and a golden mane. Nevertheless, we have no difficulty understanding and appreciating the reality of what is being said – as long, of course, as the metaphor itself is from our range of experience: a person who has no idea of what a lion is will be at a major disadvantage!

As with normal, everyday speech, the Bible uses a great deal of figurative language. The first thing we need to do is to let the words speak for themselves in all their variety and richness. Figurative language is not necessarily difficult and obscure language, even when it is used in a book like the Book of Revelation.

EXAMPLES

Let's take a few examples of metaphorical language and see how well we get on before applying what we learn to the text of Philippians, and perhaps we will see that it is often not as difficult as we might think.

Many times in the Old Testament the Promised Land is described as **'a land flowing with milk and honey'**.[3] Are we to take this description literally, or spiritually, or metaphorically?

Let's try a literal interpretation: when Israel crossed the Jordan into the Promised Land under Joshua's leadership, they were met with a vast sticky mess flowing down the main road towards them. This is very unlikely!

What about a spiritual interpretation? The land was full of the milk of the word of God and the honey of the Holy Spirit? That is stretching things a little! There is nothing either in the text, or the wider context to justify such an interpretation.

It is of course metaphorical language, telling us that it was a rich and fertile land.

Before leaving the example, however, it would be useful to think about the individual elements of the description and to ask where exactly the metaphor lies.

- **Land**: literal or metaphorical? Literal.
- **Milk and honey**: literal or metaphorical? Literal in the sense that there were real cows and real bees.
  Metaphorical in the sense that milk and honey are representative symbols of a wealth of good things.
- **Flowing**: literal or metaphorical? Metaphorical: lands don't flow, although of course milk and honey do!

[1] Collins Compact English Dictionary, HarperCollins, 1998, p534

[2] Robertson McQuilkin, Understanding and Applying the Bible, Revised Ed, Moody, 1992, p166

[3] For example, Exodus 3:8

So it is a quite sophisticated sentence in which there is a mixture of literal elements and metaphorical elements. This is one of the things that makes language so rich, and yet at the same time no-one could reasonably sustain the view that such language is obscure and impossible to understand.

In this particular example, the metaphor is chiefly carried by the verb, which indeed is often the case. In addition, the choice of the verb **'flowing'** is more precise than we may at first realise. To speak of a land **churning** with milk and honey, or **seething** with milk and honey, or **dribbling** with milk and honey would change the meaning, and in some cases quite radically. **Flowing** emphasises the richness of the supply, whereas **churning** or **seething** would add a more violent, almost sinister aspect. **Dribbling** would convey the opposite of **flowing.**

METAPHOR AND REALITY

Let's think some more about this. Suppose someone were to say, "I was stuck to the phone all day today." Once again it is not hard to spot the metaphor: **stuck.** The person doesn't mean, of course, that he spent the entire day with a telephone literally glued to his ear, unable to remove it. But the experience of being stuck, in the sense of the telephone constantly ringing and demanding his attention, was very real.

The point is this: **we use the metaphor to describe a reality.** For a metaphor to work, it has to be a metaphor of something.

Let's take this a step further: in Revelation 20, for example, we read of an angel with a chain who binds the dragon. Is the chain literal? Very unlikely. But the restraint that the angel applies to the dragon is real. This restraint is symbolised by a chain because that means something to us: we know what chains are. If the restraint exercised by the mighty angel were to be described to us as what it consists of in reality, probably none of us would have the vocabulary or frame of reference with which to understand it.

Let's think of an example of this from the everyday experience of explaining complex issues to small children. Supposing we are explaining to a child why it is important to take his time over his food and not to bolt it down. We might say that when his eyes see the food, the brain **sends a message** down to his stomach to get ready to receive the incoming supply. The child might imagine a tiny messenger on a motorbike racing between his head and his stomach, or someone sitting at mission control speaking to space station stomach! As adults we know that it is a question of electro-chemical interactions. But we don't explain it that way to a child: we use picture language to describe a reality that is impossible fully to describe at a child's level.

We should not, therefore, be surprised if, in order to explain complex, spiritual and eternal truth, God expresses himself in symbol and imagery. His purpose is not to make simple things obscure, but to make things that would otherwise be obscure to us as clear as possible to a finite human mind.

Let's listen to C S Lewis on this:

> *...very often when we are talking about something which is not perceptible by the five senses, we use words which, in one of their meanings, refer to things or actions that are. When a man says that he grasps an argument he is using a*

verb (grasp) which literally means to take something in the hands, but he is certainly not thinking that his mind has hands or that an argument can be seized like a gun. To avoid the word grasp he may change the form of expression and say, 'I see your point,' but he does not mean that a pointed object has appeared in his visual field. He may have a third shot and say, 'I follow you,' but he does not mean that he is walking behind you along a road. Everyone is familiar with this linguistic phenomenon and the grammarians call it metaphor. But it is a serious mistake to think that metaphor is an optional thing which poets and authors may put into their work as a decoration and plain speakers can do without. The truth is that if we are going to talk at all about things which are not perceived by the senses, we are forced to use language metaphorically. [4]

[4] C S Lewis, *Miracles*, Collins, Fontana Books, 1947, p 76

We must let language be language, in all its depth and variety, and apply the normal rules of speech which we use every day, rather than jumping to the conclusion that the Bible by definition contains a special kind of religious language and imagery which is impossible to understand.

METAPHOR AND CODE

A final point about figurative and symbolic language before we turn once more to Philippians. Let's think of a wonderful description Chapter 5 of the Book of Revelation gives us of the throne of God. John notices a scroll in the right hand of the occupant of the throne, but then it appears to him that there is no one worthy to open the scroll. He begins to weep, but is told not to because, "the lion of the tribe of Judah ... has triumphed. He is able to open the scroll..." [5]

[5] Revelation 5:5

If we ask who is the Lion of the tribe of Judah, it is clear that the answer is the Lord Jesus Christ. We are then told that John turns round and sees a Lamb. Who is the Lamb? The answer is clearly the same: the Lord Jesus Christ. So, we conclude, this is a kind of code:

- lion   = the Lord Jesus.
- lamb   = the Lord Jesus.

But why bother using a code at all if the solution to it is so obvious? The answer is that it is not a code. There are a few occasions where the Bible does use a kind of code – the number 666, we are told, is the number of man. [6] This is rare, and it is not what is happening here.

[6] Revelation 13:18

If we approach the use of metaphorical language as if it is simply or even mainly about deciphering a code, we have missed the point almost entirely. The images of 'lion' and 'lamb' are deliberately selected not as code but as metaphor, because they reflect attributes of Christ that would be hard to express any other way, and certainly hard to express so vividly.

- **Lion**: majestic king, the Lord in all his magnificent power.
- **Lamb**: meek, gentle, submissive (and yet strong: he has seven horns). We also should add to this the background of the Passover Lamb (Exodus 12) and the Old Testament sacrificial system, which together add depth and significance to this particular metaphor.

We can note also that the contrast between the two images of lion and lamb adds further depth and impact. This is a description of the Lord which fires our imagination - we are not simply told in neat theological propositions that Jesus is pure, wise, all-powerful and yet meek. The Bible does that, but it does more and we need to allow the figurative language of the Bible to speak in all its power.

The fact is that we will lose part of the immense richness of the Bible if we treat its symbolic language simply as code in the sense of 'A = 6', or 'D = green'. Most of us, and not just children, think more easily in terms of pictures.

THE NEED TO EXERCISE CONTROL

Having said that, it is important that we exercise control in how we interpret figurative language. While metaphor must mean something, it can not mean anything. There are some who tend to approach figurative language as if it can mean anything that they want it to say. Some Christian teachers have been guilty of very fanciful interpretation. In addition, this is where sects and cults tend to go wrong, particularly in their approach to the Book of Revelation.[7] As a result of these extremes, some have reacted in the opposite direction to the extent of virtually ignoring the Bible's use of metaphor, fearful of any use of spiritual imagination.

Once again, we should be guided by context and by what is made clear and explicit elsewhere in the Bible.[8] The Bible is its own best interpreter. If, for example, we return to Revelation's use of the 'lamb' metaphor for Christ, we will find that numerous references in the Old Testament make it clear how we should understand the term. In passages such as Isaiah 40:11, Isaiah 53:7 and Jeremiah 51:40, lambs are associated with gentleness, innocence and submissiveness. In addition, "Lambs are specifically mentioned in connection with sacrifices more than eighty times in Exodus, Leviticus and Numbers."[9]

In particular, it is important and helpful to note how the New Testament writers use Old Testament symbols and images. For example, the letter to the Hebrews makes extensive use of the system of sacrifices and service to God associated with the Tabernacle. The often complex and detailed arrangements under the Old Covenant are referred to by the writer as "a copy and shadow of heavenly things" (Hebrews 8:5). As a **copy** of heavenly realities, they symbolised key spiritual truths for the people at the time. As a **shadow**, they pointed forward to their fulfilment in Christ and as such they are of great value to us today in giving us a visual understanding of the person and achievement of the Lord Jesus. Hebrews gives us considerable guidance as to how we should interpret such Old Testament symbols, so that we are not left to the subjective flights of fancy of our own imaginations. We will look at this in much more detail later in this guide when we consider how we should interpret the Old Testament.

[7] See for example Messianic Revolution, by David Katz and Richard H Popkin, Penguin, 1998, for a secular account of this feature, and especially their discussion of the Waco incident (Texas, April 1995) amongst others in Chapter 8.

[8] A most helpful guide in this area is the Dictionary of Biblical Imagery, IVP, 1998, edited by Leland Ryken, James C Wilhoit and Tremper Longman III.

[9] Dictionary of Biblical Imagery, p 484

FIGURATIVE LANGUAGE IN PHILIPPIANS

In common with other New Testament books, Philippians has its share of figurative language. This is another time when a good commentary can be very useful, because some of the metaphor is lost in translation. An example of this is found in Philippians 1:8 which NIV translates as "I long for all of you with the affection of Christ Jesus." In the original Greek, the vivid metaphor of 'entrails' or 'inner parts' is used. Gordon Fee comments helpfully: "...probably because of the physical, deeply visceral, internal 'feelings' that one sometimes experiences in the emotion of deep affection for another."[10]

[10] Fee, op cit, p 94

An example of a similar kind of thing is found in the previous verse which the NIV translates as "I have you in my heart." In common with the Greeks and the Jews, even in the technologically advanced West we use parts of our physical bodies in a figurative sense. We give someone a hand; we put our back into our work; we have no stomach for a fight; we put our foot in it! It is colourful and effective language used to express a reality which is not difficult to understand, and at the same time to enhance our appreciation of that reality. In the example of Philippians 1:8, the strong image used effectively conveys the remarkable compassion of Paul for other believers.

With all of this in mind it is time to do some work of our own! Take time now to think through the following words and expressions in their context, both to work out their basic meaning and to appreciate the richness and impact of the metaphors Paul uses.

- 2:3, 5; 3:7, 8   counting

- 3:2   dogs

- 3:8   dung/refuse/rubbish

- 3:19   those whose god is their belly

- 1:11; 4: 17   fruit or harvest

- 4:19   God's riches in glory

Careful reading through the text will reveal additional metaphors, but this will get you started.

WORD STUDIES

The technological revolution, and particularly the world of computing, has brought with it a vast array of new words and concepts. A depressing feature of this, for those of us who are older than we think, is the ease with which young people, even those of primary school age, master the new terminology. As with any new area of experience, let alone a new language, unless we make an effort to understand these words and concepts we will feel forever shut out.

It should be no great surprise that the Bible contains a number of key terms which may be new to us: **sin, church, redemption, grace, justification, sacrifice, faith, propitiation, holiness**. These are the 'big words' of the Bible, and the more we read it, the more we will see that grasping the meaning of these words is vital to getting the message of the Bible.

Of course all the words in the Bible, as originally given by God, are inspired, but not all of them carry the same weight of meaning. Most words will be relatively straightforward and we should not get the impression that we need to study intensively every single word of every single sentence. However in addition to the big words, as we read and re-read a paragraph, we will come across words that are obviously key to correct and full understanding of the message. Often we will find that these words are repeated or unusual in some way, or difficult. In these cases we will need to take time to study these individual words in more detail.

Our main objective in such word studies is **to understand what the biblical authors meant by the use of a particular key word in a particular context**.

Such word studies are rewarding and can even be fun to do, but before going through the core process involved in an effective word study, it is wise to be aware that a number of 'banana skins' await the unwary.

BANANA SKIN 1 – RELYING ON THE ENGLISH

Unless you are using an original language edition, **the Bible in your hand is a translation**. English translations often will use different words in different contexts to translate the same original language word. It will be no surprise, for example, to discover that there are two major Greek words translated by the English word 'new' and they have different nuances of meaning. The reverse is also true: different original language words can be translated using the same English word. For example the English word 'perfect' is used to translate seven different Greek words! [1]

It follows from this that if we want to study a particular key word, we should not simply rely on the number of times it occurs in our English translation. We need to get behind our English translation to make sure that we are studying a key word or concept as it is used in the original language. To do this we do not need to know New Testament Greek, although it would be a considerable help. But we will need to learn how to use a concordance (see later) which lists all the occurrences of each original language word.

BANANA SKIN 2 – I KNOW WHAT THIS MEANS

It is likely that we will have some ideas in our mind as to what these key words mean. Some of our ideas may be exactly right, and some may be completely wrong, and some will fall somewhere between the two extremes. We should be wary of deciding the meaning in advance and then of seeking to impose that meaning on each use of the word.

BANANA SKIN 3 – IT ALWAYS MEANS...

The fact is that **one word can have a considerable range of meaning.** Think of the English word **new**: it can mean *recently made* (as in a new car), even though the design has been around a long time; it can mean new in the sense of *never before existing*, totally novel; it can mean new in the sense of *additional* (a new coin for your collection). The precise meaning will largely depend on the precise context as we will presently illustrate from Paul's use of the term **flesh** both in Philippians and widely in the New Testament.

When we work out what a particular word means in one context, it does not necessarily follow that it will mean the same in every context, any more than 'new' means the same in every context . Nor does it follow that it will carry all the meanings each time it is used. **Context is the key**.

BANANA SKIN 4 –ROOTS AND SHOOTS

Sometimes it can be helpful to discover the origin of a particular word and its constituent parts. Often it is not. Words change in their meaning. Even when we know how a certain word was used in secular Greek, it does not necessarily imply that it means precisely the same in the New Testament. There can be no substitute for studying how the biblical writers themselves use words in particular contexts. Once again **context is key.**

The opposite problem – **shoots** – is where we read modern meaning back into the ancient text. As D A Carson points out, just because the Greek word 'dynamis' lies behind the English word 'dynamite', does not mean that Paul had explosives in mind when he tells us in Romans 1:16 that the gospel is "the power (dynamis) of God unto salvation." [2] Paul knew nothing of Semtex or TNT.

[1] See McQuilkin, op cit, p 115

[2] D A Carson, Exegetical Fallacies, p34

DOING A WORD STUDY

The major steps in the process of understanding key Bible words are as follows:

1. Select the key word/concept you wish to study – for example **flesh** in Philippians 3:3

2. Establish the Greek word that is translated here as **flesh**

3. Find out the range of meaning of the Greek word, using a concordance and/or dictionary of Bible words

4. Study the word in its immediate context and in the wider context of the letter as a whole – the concordance will give you all occurrences of the Greek word in Philippians

5. Consider the main uses of the word in other New Testament books to see if this casts further light on Paul's usage of the word in Philippians

6. Establish your conclusions regarding what **flesh** means in Philippians 3, and check this against a good commentary

USING A CONCORDANCE

A concordance is a list of all the words used in a particular literary work, giving the context of each occurrence and, usually, the meaning. Sometimes an edition of the Bible will have a short concordance at the end. While this is useful – especially if you have nothing else – you need to remember that it is a **short** version and will only include selected references.

It is important that, if possible, you use the concordance that matches the version of the Bible you are using. For the NIV I use the *Zondervan NIV Exhaustive Concordance*. If you have a concordance that has been around your house for some time, the chances are it is based on the KJV. It is still possible to use it, but the process will be a little more complicated if your main study Bible is the NIV or the NASB, or some other version:

- First, look up the particular verse in the **KJV** to find out what English word it selects for the **NIV** word you want to study

- Then follow the procedure below

Let's return to the word we have already selected: **flesh**.

Step 1. Look up the word in the first section of the concordance. You will find FLESH followed by a number in parenthesis – in this case 130. That means that the NIV has used this English word 130 times in both Old and New Testaments. Usually a list of related words is given, but there are none for 'flesh'.

Step 2. Find the reference to the verse in Philippians in which we have found the word **flesh**. Books of the Bible are listed in the order in which they appear, Old Testament before New, with the result that any Philippians entries will come towards the end of the long list of 130. We find three references in Philippians set out as follows:

Php	3:2	those mutilators of the **f.**	NIG
	3:3	and who put no confidence in the **f**_	4922
	3:4	to put confidence in the **f:**	4922

The 'Php' that heads this section tells us that the book in which the occurrences of the word are found is Philippians. What follows is what is known as the context line. On each line the first number indicates the location in the book. For example, '3:2' means Philippians Chapter 3, verse 2. This is followed by the part of the NIV verse that contains the key word, thus giving us the immediate context. The position of the key word is indicated by its first letter highlighted in bold – here it is **f.**
The final column may seem a bit of a mystery, especially as in one case there are letters and in the other cases numbers. The letters NIG stand for 'not in Greek' (guess what NIH would stand for?) and mean that the translators have used a word in English which has no exact equivalent in the original language. The numbers refer to the Dictionary-Index.

Step 3. Look up the number from the final column in the Greek to English Dictionary and Index towards the end of the concordance. In the case of the word **flesh** the number is 4922. There we will be told that the Greek word used in Philippians 3:3 is **sarx**. The 'n.' that follows indicates that **sarx** is a noun, and the number in parenthesis – here 147 – tells us that this word occurs 147 times in the New Testament.

Step 4. Establish the word's range of meaning. The concordance gives us this definition of what the word means in the New Testament: "flesh, body, the soft tissue of a creature, often in contrast to bone, ligament, or sinew; by extension human, humankind, with a focus on the fallen human nature, which is frail and corrupt in contrast to immaterial (spiritual things), thus the NIV translation 'sinful nature'".[3] The concordance then gives us a list of how the NIV has translated the word in the New Testament, and how often each translation occurs.

[3] NIV Exhaustive Concordance, p 1590

[Possible Step 5. We can use the Concordance to trace the same concept in the Old Testament, once again to see if this might provide some helpful background information. We discover that the index number for the most common Hebrew word that is translated **flesh** in the NIV is 1414.]

All of this is very helpful. We have identified the original Greek word, we have found details of the semantic range of the Greek word and how it has been translated in various contexts in the New Testament. By following the number 4922, in the listing under **flesh**, we have discovered many (but not all) of the contexts in which the word **sarx** is used. If we want to conduct a wider study, we can look up the other English words used by the NIV to translate **sarx** and study those contexts.

A dictionary of New Testament words will also help us here, both in giving us definitions and explanations for how the word is used, and by listing the occurrences of the Greek word in the New Testament.

The better commentaries will often provide additional details to help us grasp the full significance of important words.

A FINAL WORD

Sometimes authors and Bible teachers can make mistakes with word studies, usually slipping on one of the banana skins we have mentioned! Before leaving the word **sarx**, for example, note that the NIV sometimes translates it as **sinful nature**, for example Galatians 5:13, or Romans 7:25. This is more of a statement of how the translators believe the word is used than it is a translation of it. The words that mean **sinful** and **nature** do not appear in the original Greek. Now let's suppose that we were doing a study on what the New Testament teaches about human nature. If we relied solely on the NIV English translation, and did not check the concordance, we might easily think that Paul refers often to the concept of 'nature' in Romans 6 and 7, for example, when in fact he never mentions it.

An appeal to the Greek is not always a guarantee of accurate interpretation, as this illustration from Haddon Robinson indicates:

> For instance sermons on "How to know the will of God" advance the thesis that "Inward peace gives assurance of God's direction in our decisions." Colossians 3:15, "And let the peace of Christ rule in your hearts," is offered in support of that idea. Since every word of Scripture is God-breathed, the preacher provides a word study of braxzeo "to rule" or "to umpire". Christ's peace, the sermon goes, serves as a referee who "calls" each decision we make. When a Christian lives within God's will, he experiences peace which "surpasses all comprehension". Through this peace the referee, Christ, affirms our correct decisions. Should Christians make wrong choices, they will experience inner anxiety – a sign that they have stepped out of God's will.
> Such an approach has the ring of exposition. If focuses on the Greek text and sounds extremely practical. Unfortunately it is not biblical. A reading of the context reveals that Paul is not talking about decision making, but instead about how Christians should relate to one another. T K Abbott comments that the phrase peace of Christ "is not to inward peace of the soul but to peace with one another as the context shows." Using Colossians 3:15 to preach on God's guidance ignores completely the idea the apostle intended. When sermons proceed from such a cavalier handling of the Bible, they divorce sound hermeneutics from homiletics. [4]

[4] Haddon Robinson, Making a Difference in Preaching, Baker Books 1999, pp 72,73

13 APPLYING THE MESSAGE

The process of Bible study is often organised under three headings:

- observation
- interpretation
- application

In practice it is hard to separate them into totally discrete processes, but it is helpful to be aware of their distinct emphases. The first is to do with **seeing what is there**, the second to do with **understanding what we see**, and the third is to do with **applying what we understand**.

We started out in this guide with a variety of questions designed primarily to help us **observe** correctly. This goes a little against the grain in an instant society where folks want to get to the 'bottom line' as quickly as possible. Culture in the West has changed, with increasing emphasis on experience, less interest in theory and more interest in what works. As a result, there is a tendency amongst those who are serious about following Christ to rush to the application stage – to see 'what's in it for me.' And the missing ingredient is often not interpretation but observation.

We tend, for a variety of reasons, not to see (in the sense of really notice) what is there, and substitute for it what is not there! My brother used to quote some corrupted words of a well-known children's hymn:

Wonderful things in the Bible I see,
Some put there by you and some put there by me!

Observing what the author actually says – as opposed to what we think he says, or what we would like him to say – is the critical first step to our whole endeavour, and for that reason if the emphasis of this guide lies anywhere it lies here.

At the same time, the observation stage has involved looking for links between ideas, for key themes, for thought-flow. This inevitably involves increasing amounts of **interpretation**, and we have devoted considerable space to some important principles of accurate understanding of the message.

Now we need to think in more detail about **application**.

ALL SCRIPTURE IS PROFITABLE AND PRACTICAL

Paul's statement to Timothy guides us here: "All Scripture is inspired by God and is profitable for teaching, reproof, correction and training in righteousness, so that the man (woman) of God might be fully equipped for every good work." (2 Timothy 3:16)

All Scripture is not only inspired but is **profitable. All Scripture**. That includes Ezekiel and Leviticus. It means the instructions for the construction of the Tabernacle, the genealogies, the complex prophecies. All is profitable.

WHAT DO WE MEAN BY PRACTICAL?

We need to be careful that we don't narrow our understanding of how Scripture applies to the search for a moral to a story, or to a variety of lists: a list of lessons we can learn, a list of things that we must do, or avoid doing. While it is often helpful to think, for example, how a particular teaching might apply to our marriage, or to how we control our tongues, much of Scripture does not fit into our neat categories, indicating at least that there is much more to the application of Scripture than this.

All Scripture is **profitable for teaching**. Not simply teaching moral lessons, but teaching the truth that sets us free: the truth about God, about the origins and purpose of human life, about the human condition, about God's solution in Christ.

Paul in Romans 12 teaches us that we are to be transformed by the renewal of our minds, the renewal of our thinking.[33] The application of Scripture to us, therefore, will frequently be at the level of changing how we think: changing our values, our mindset and worldview.

[33] Romans 12:1,2

Or at least it should be. Often we replace true transformation with the attempt to get ourselves or others to conform to particular standards or rules which we know to be right. But such conformation can be very artificial and external, depending much more on personal disciplines and human technique than on the operation of God's Spirit within us. We will only be truly transformed if we are transformed from the inside out. And the Spirit works through the Word of God to teach us, to inform our thinking, to challenge and change how we look at life, resulting in behavioural change.

At the heart of Christianity is a relationship with the living God. Reading his word is not like reading a book of management techniques, a self-help guide, a car manual or guide to gourmet cooking. We read the Word to discern God's voice, to encounter him. This builds, strengthens and expands our relationship in ways that simply cannot (and must not) be reduced to 'the six keys to a successful walk with God'.

Let me use an analogy to explain what I mean. I try to spend as much time as I can with my wife and my children, and find that it is tremendously rewarding. After an hour or two with my wife I don't ask what the application point is! (Although there is no doubt that I learn a lot when I listen to her, and it sometimes even leads to change on my part!) And I have discovered that I do things to please my wife NOT because she gives me a 'to do' list – although her occasional lists are very helpful – but because I love her, and even more because remarkably and wonderfully she loves me.

Having sat through too many abstract and deadly dull Bible talks, I understand what folks mean when they say that they need practical Bible teaching. However, we need to be careful that we do not define 'practical' too narrowly in terms of 'to do' lists, or we can end up replacing relationship with legalism.

When Paul shares his motivation for service, he tells us that the love of Christ constrains him. The commands and lists of Scripture are vital guides for us as to what constitutes right and holy living that pleases the Lord. But our motivation to live like this does not come from reading lists; it comes from our devotion to Christ, from our experience of his compassion and love, and from his revelation of his purposes to us. That is why, when Paul appeals to the Philippians to serve harmoniously together, he does so on the grounds of their shared experience of the love of Christ.

Much of Scripture is designed to reveal Christ to us – such as, for example, Philippians 2 – for it is out of our devotion and loyalty to Christ as supreme Lord, Saviour, forgiver and director of our lives that we will increasingly seek to please him. So while reading material on witnessing, for example, can be a wonderful guide, the motivation to witness stems directly from our enthusiasm and passion for Christ. Otherwise it so easily becomes another thing on an evangelical 'to do' list and can quickly turn into guilt motivated legalism.

Those passages, therefore, where our chief take away is, "Wow, isn't God utterly amazing?", are the most practical.

We should be wary of the habit some writers and Bible teachers have of making a division in Paul's letters between the 'doctrinal part' and the 'practical part'. I think I know what they mean, but it is potentially a very misleading division. **All Scripture is profitable**, and not just those parts that contain explicit directives for how we should live.

Belief behaves, truth transforms. All Scripture is profitable for teaching, reproof, correction and training in righteousness. We do not naturally either think the way God thinks, or live the way God would have us live. We need to hear and understand the truth – we need the doctrines, we need the presentation of truth, we need the teaching, for this will challenge our thinking, expose the error and lead us back to the true path.

WE HAVE A PROBLEM

Everybody has a problem, and most people have many. As a result, when it comes to understanding where and how Scripture applies, often we come to it not as listeners but as people who are seeking answers to our specific problems. This is good to a point, but I need to sit back for a moment and realise that the supreme purpose of Scripture was not problem solving in my life!

The Bible is God's revelation of himself to us. Our primary approach must be to

allow God to set the topic of conversation and establish the agenda. Where our approach is conditioned by our 'problems', we can so easily miss what is actually being said and shape the text according to our own needs. In addition, the problems that we think we have may not at all be the problems we really have. How we see life, our definition of happiness, our ambitions and values may all be seriously at fault, thus impairing our judgement. We need first to listen to God and to see all of life (including ourselves) through his eyes, from the perspective of the priorities of the eternal kingdom of God, rather than from the perspective of our own problems.

I once attended a series of studies on the Book of Acts in which the teacher had decided that the text was to be read as a 'Manual of Christian Ministry', with the result that in every passage we were asked to uncover the 'ministry principles' involved. Certainly some helpful insights emerged, because some passages in Acts can be looked at this way. However, techniques of ministry are not primarily what Acts is about. The result of the teacher's approach was an increasingly superficial reading of the book, where we were searching for lists, for 'the moral to this tale' type applications, rather than allowing the text to speak for itself. The meaning of large chunks of text was almost entirely missed because they did not fit the grid the teacher had imposed upon it.

It is surely only good manners to let God speak and establish the agenda for us. It also makes sense, for he knows what we need to think about much better than we do. He is always practical!

BRIDGING THE APPLICATION GAP

We have already considered the application of Scripture to our thinking and living in terms of its presentation of timeless truth, which is not bound in any way by being addressed to specific individuals or to a specific circumstance within a specific culture.

However, with each passage of Scripture that we are studying, it IS important to bear in mind the following questions:

- To whom was this written/originally spoken?

- To what degree is what is written conditioned by history, local culture and specific circumstances?

- How different is that culture from ours?

TO WHOM WAS PHILIPPIANS WRITTEN?

It is an important first step when it comes to application to ask: **What did this mean to the original audience? How did it apply to them?**

Answering these questions will help us to see how much of what is said is bound up with local culture and specific circumstances.

Philippians was written to believers in Jesus Christ living in Philippi two thousand years ago. There are certain specifics that relate to the original audience and in that sense separate us from them:

- They had sent a gift to Paul

- They knew Timothy and Epaphroditus

- Many of them had witnessed Paul's imprisonment in Philippi, had heard him speak, had shared meals and jokes with him

- There was a strong bond of affection between the church at Philippi and Paul. He knew many of them, prayed for them by name, loved them to the point of laying down his life for them

- The culture and historical circumstances of Philippi were markedly different from our own: Rome was the superpower, not the US; Christianity was on the increase – it was a pre-Christian society, whereas many Western societies are now very much post-Christian

In a real sense we are **listening in** to a conversation between Paul and his friends at Philippi, a conversation shaped by a particular cultural and historical setting. The better we understand that cultural and historical setting, the better we will grasp the meaning of the letter. The more we take into account the impact their personal history with Paul would have had on them as they read the letter, the deeper our appreciation of the text will be, even if we cannot experience this impact in exactly the same way.

While this is so, we must not exaggerate the width of the gap that separates us from this 1st Century church. The fact that this letter was addressed to the believers in Philippi does not rule out its application to us today. This is divinely inspired apostolic teaching. God intended it not just for them but for us – it is not simply an interesting piece of historical correspondence. This is God's Word to us as we likewise seek to follow and serve Jesus Christ. While one or two details are very specific to the Philippians – their gift to Paul, the actions of Epaphroditus on their behalf, the 'warring sisters' – what we have in this letter is timeless teaching fleshed out in real situations. Far from the personal (to the Philippians) nature of the letter being a barrier, it is a positive advantage, earthing God's truth in human experience.

Philippians was also written specifically to the **elders and deacons** at Philippi. This is a helpful guide to us in our application. This does not mean that if you are not an elder or deacon there is nothing here for you – leaders are meant to be examples of godly living for the rest of us to follow. It does mean that Philippians has specific application to issues of service and leadership.

Rather than being a barrier to our understanding, the identification of the specific audience is an important guide both to interpretation and application. There is very little in Philippians that could reasonably be said to be exclusively limited to the original audience. The teaching is timeless, but given personal roots and shape through the specifics of author, audience and named characters.

SIN IS STILL SIN

In addition, the fact is that **the condition of the human heart has not changed**: human selfishness, alienation and rebellion remain the same. While the context in which these things express themselves has changed, sin is still sin; adultery, greed, pride and anger are no less real now than they were then. Advances in science and technology, while bringing many benefits, furnish human beings with ever more sophisticated means of sinning, rather than solutions to greed and selfishness!

Consider, for example, the warning in Philippians 3 concerning those whose **god is their belly** and whose **mind is on earthly things**.[1] The way in which people today demonstrate that their values and thinking are totally earth-bound in my own city of Belfast may be rather different from how it was in Philippi – fast cars and electronic entertainment were not around in Paul's day. But the underlying sins are the same – a definition of life based on seeing this world as the only world, denying either the reality or the relevance of the eternal kingdom of God.

Let's take a few more examples from Philippians.

[1] Philippians 3:19

- Paul states that he hopes to send Timothy to them soon (2:19). This has no direct application to us. It is almost two thousand years since Paul sent Timothy anywhere! However we can learn something from the reason Paul sought to send Timothy to them: so that he might be encouraged by Timothy's news about how the folks at Philippi are doing. And no doubt Timothy in turn could encourage them in taking to heart Paul's teaching to them. This evidence of ongoing care, the desire to know how people are doing spiritually, the practical steps Paul and Timothy were prepared to take in times when travel and communications were neither quick nor easy – all this conveys important spiritual principles, and in particular for leaders.

- Paul wrote this letter in part to urge them to deal with a specific problem they faced in the church: the conflict between Euodia and Syntyche (Chapter 4). Paul did not invent the incident in order to teach timeless principles of conflict resolution. The event happened, two thousand years ago, centred on two actual, living, breathing human beings. In one sense it has nothing to do with us. It is their story, not ours. Yet, in dealing with this specific historical incident, Paul points them to some vital and universally valid spiritual truths which have much application to us.

- In Chapter 3 Paul warns about 'dogs', the judaizers who proved to be a significant problem in the early church, through their misunderstanding and misapplication of the Law in general and circumcision in particular. Now I have yet to come across anyone who has urged upon me the necessity of circumcision if I wish to be truly accepted by God. That does not mean that what Paul says here is irrelevant to us and has no application. Far from it. What it does mean is that instead of looking for a direct equivalent in our own world we need to discern what the values and attributes of these 'dogs' were, and see if anything similar manifests itself in our own situation. Some of these – misunderstanding of the purposes and role of the Law, confidence in human achievement, wrongful pride in education, religious snobbery, dependence on personal zeal – are certainly realities in my context. Rebellious, self-confident religious 'flesh' still manifests itself in many ways in our different contexts.

Some of the time, therefore, when we are seeking to make specific applications within our own context we need to follow this simple process:

- What did this mean to its original audience?
- What are the underlying spiritual truths?
- How do these truths apply to us in our context?

EXPLICIT DIRECTIVES

Often there is little or no filter of culture to work through. The core principles are frequently set out for us in the form of **explicit directives which apply to all people at all times.**

[2] Philippians 2:12

- When Paul tells the Philippians to "work out your salvation" ,[2]this applies directly to us. The cultural context in which we work it out may be very different, but the principle and command are the same.

[3] Philippians 2:2

- When he tells them to be "like-minded, having the same love, being one in spirit and purpose",[3] we cannot avoid the direct application to us by saying that this simply applied to the Philippians. The whole context of Chapter 2 tells us that these are attributes that we are all to have.

[4] Philippians 4:6

- When he tells them "Do not be anxious" [4], it is true that some of the things that caused greatest anxiety for the folks at Philippi may not be a feature in our lives. Yet anxiety is a reality, and very much so for leaders (elders and deacons) who are caught up in a situation where Christian workers have fallen out with each other. This also has direct application to our modern contexts.

THE POWER OF EXAMPLE

On other occasions the core **principles are expressed through example.**

[5] Philippians 2:25-30

- In Chapter 2 we are given the example of Epaphroditus. He risked his life in bringing the gift from the Philippian church to Paul. We may never be called upon to imitate his actions exactly. But the very clear implication is that we are called upon to imitate his heart, for Paul says that such people should be welcomed with joy and held in high esteem.[5]

The context itself will often guide us as to what these examples illustrate. In the case of Epaphroditus, it is clear that he is given as an example of someone who is demonstrating the mind and attitude of Christ, which is the main subject of Philippians 2.

We need to be careful to allow **the context of the example** to shape our application and not let imagination run away with us. There are times when Scripture relates incidents to us with little or nothing by means of explicit statement of the key principle being taught. Almost always this will be clear when we consider the wider context in which the incident is recorded.

In addition, it is wise always to check the principle(s) and application(s) we have deduced from a text **against what is explicitly taught elsewhere in Scripture**. God does not contradict himself. If the principle we derive from our reading of what Paul says about Epaphroditus is not clearly taught elsewhere; or, even more worrying, if it contradicts what is explicitly taught elsewhere, we need to revise our understanding!

This is particularly true when it comes to considering the events recorded in the Book of Acts. All kinds of personal experiences are recorded, such as how it was that the Samaritans received the Holy Spirit.[6] We need to be careful not to build our doctrine of how folks receive the Spirit on the basis of this incident. If we do we will find that our theory is contradicted by how others received the Spirit in the early chapters of Acts, and by what the apostles teach about the Holy Spirit in the letters. We must allow the New Testament to interpret the experiences for us rather than form our own theories based on our reading of Luke's historical account.

[6] Acts 8:4-25

THE ANTITHESIS PRINCIPLE

To understand the contemporary relevance and specific application of a particular biblical truth I have found it exceptionally helpful to apply **the antithesis principle**.

This is based on the assumption that **for every core truth (thesis) of Scripture, there is its opposite false teaching (antithesis) somewhere within the cultural mindset, not just of Paul's day but of our own.**

Satan is utterly and implacably opposed to God and his truth. He is the Deceiver and the Father of lies who orchestrates the fashions of thinking that prevail in our various cultures. Before submitting to the Lordship of Christ, according to Paul we are enemies in our minds towards God [7], we follow the ways of this world and of the ruler of the kingdom of the air; we live according to the dictates of the desires and thoughts of our sinful nature.[8]

[7] Colossians 1:21

[8] Ephesians 2:2,3

Over against this sophisticated and sinister fabric of lies stands the truth of Christ. To put this another way: **the gospel challenges all cultures, especially our own.**

Sometimes **this antithesis will take the shape of a very strong, 'in your face' denial of biblical truth.** Remember the Serpent's bold statement to Eve: "you will not surely die" [9] This was a flat and dramatic contradiction of God's word to them, similar to the rejection of the idea of a God who judges, or the rejection of restraint on personal indulgence that Paul describes in those who are enemies of the cross in Philippians 3.

[9] Genesis 3:4

On other occasions **the antithesis will be something that looks like the truth, but isn't.** In the same confrontation, Satan backed up his denial of God's word with a statement that was **in itself true**, for when he said, "your eyes will be opened, and you will be like God, knowing good and evil" [10], that part was true.[11] We can imagine the judaizers of Philippians quoting Old Testament Scripture and sounding very spiritual, but they actually were opponents of the gospel. Lies are always dangerous; the more truth they contain, the more dangerous they become.

[10] Genesis 3:5
[11] See Genesis 3:7, 22

Time and time again Jesus pointed up this clash of thinking, of values, most notably perhaps in the 'upside down' wisdom of the Sermon on the Mount: "Happy are those who mourn... happy are the meek... happy are you when people insult you, persecute you and falsely say all kinds of evil against you..." [12] We think, for example, of how he taught that the self-saving life ends up in total loss, whereas the self-giving life for Christ's sake and the gospel ends up with truly finding life. If we want to see how the message of Christ applies to our life today, it will help us to look for the points of tension and of head-on collision between God's kingdom and the mindset and values of this present age.

[12] Matthew 5:1-12

Once again let's look at a few examples in Philippians:

- Chapter 1: **Paul stresses his confidence in God who is able to finish what he has started.**
  * Contemporary society talks a great deal about confidence – whole books are written about it. But it is confidence in ourselves, in human abilities and achievement. There is a major clash of focus here.

- Chapter 1: **Paul talks positively about suffering for the gospel.**
  * Contemporary Western culture has little in the way of category for suffering. It is to be avoided at all costs: life is organised around the principle of our individual right to happiness, and an important ingredient in happiness is the absence of suffering.

- Chapter 1: **Paul's outlook on life enables him to see death as gain.**
  * Death is loss for contemporary society; it is the ultimate loss, because it is the end of human existence.

- Chapter 2: **Paul focuses on the servant mindset and values of Christ.**
  * His servant attitude would be much admired today, but little followed. Often those who do advocate what is called 'servant leadership' do so because it is the most effective way of gaining influence over others, not because it is right.

Why not try some of these for yourself? What might be the contemporary antithesis that would challenge each of the following teachings?

- Paul's description in Chapter 2:25-30 of the kind of person we should honour

- Paul's teaching in Chapter 3 on the surpassing value of knowing Christ in the context of his natural attainments/advantages, as many of his contemporaries would see them

- Paul's exhortation in Chapter 4 to fill our minds with things that are true, noble, pure, lovely

- Paul's teaching on contentment in Chapter 4 in the context of fluctuating financial fortune and uncertainty.

SOME USEFUL APPLICATION QUESTIONS

It would be helpful to work on **developing a set of application** questions that we consistently ask each time we are seeking to work through the implications of what Scripture teaches.

Again the New Testament will guide us here. For example, after speaking of the future judgement and destruction of the heavens and earth, Peter asks: "Since everything will be destroyed in this way, what kind of people ought you to be?"[13] Great question! To put it another way: if we were to take this truth seriously, what difference would it make?

This will take thoughtful consideration and prayer. The New Testament does not spell out every possible application in specific detail, for people and contexts are hugely different. A great example of this comes in Paul's second letter to his young friend Timothy. Even though Paul knew Timothy very well, after teaching the analogies of the soldier, the athlete and the farmer in 2 Timothy 2, he says to him: "Reflect on what I am saying, for the Lord will give you insight into all this." [14] The Holy Spirit is very interested in the way we personalise and apply the truth.

Paul does a similar thing when talking about financial giving both in 1 Corinthians 16 and 2 Corinthians 8 and 9. He resists the temptation to give a specific percentage or amount – if it was a temptation. Instead he teaches the principles and asks each individual to come to his or her own decision before the Lord (see especially 1 Corinthians 16:1 and 2 Corinthians 9:7).

Please note: I am not saying that the underlying truth changes from person to person and from culture to culture. **The truth remains the same.** It is at the level of application that there will often be differences.

Here are a few application questions that I find helpful:

- What is it about this passage or teaching that made me feel uncomfortable? Why? What do I need to do about that?

- Are there explicit directives here which I need to apply to my life?

- Are there underlying spiritual principles which I need to apply to my life?

- What are the challenges in this passage to the way I naturally think?

[13] 2 Peter 3:11

[14] 2 Timothy 2:7

- If I were to take this passage or teaching seriously, what difference would it make? How would my attitudes and values change? What would I be doing more of or less of as a result? What kind of activities would be consistent with this truth?

- How does the teaching of this passage apply to me in the context of Christian community? (NB – in the West we tend to read the New Testament very individualistically, whereas it was mostly written to communities of believers, to be worked out in the context of our connectedness in the Body of Christ.)

[15] Matthew 7:24-27

Jesus taught about the wise man who built his house on the foundation of rock.[15] We don't build by agreeing with the principle of building on rock, or by admiring the strength of the rock, or the success of others who have built on it. We build through obedience in our own lives to what God tells us to do. In the context of the startling visual parable of his washing of the disciples' feet Jesus said to them: "Now that you know these things, you will be blessed [truly happy and fulfilled] if you do them."[16]

[16] John 13:12

MOVING ON FROM HERE

By this stage you have engaged in an increasingly detailed reading of one of the books in the Bible. Only 65 more to go!

Of those 65, 19 are letters, so, having studied Philippians, we now at least have some of the key tools that we need to unlock a substantial portion of the Bible.

At the same time, there are **39** Old Testament books, none of them letters! So, from a certain point of view, we could say that the strength of our approach so far – the focus on the study of one New Testament letter – is also its weakness, for it has left all the other kinds of biblical literature virtually untouched, especially the Old Testament. Reading a letter is one thing; but how should we approach Old Testament poetry, the wisdom literature of Proverbs, the great historical books such as Samuel and Kings, the prophetic writings of Isaiah, Jeremiah, not forgetting Nehemiah's memoirs?

In addition to the wider variety of literary genre, the Old Testament poses other kinds of challenges for us:

- The Old Testament is old! Its final book was written some 400 years before the birth of Christ – almost 2500 years ago. It was also written over a period of around 1000 years, and covers a span of history much longer than that.

- It contains some very lengthy books, a challenge to the less committed reader!

- The social and cultural context is even more distant and potentially obscured than that of the New Testament.

- It was written in a different period of redemptive history – that is, it was written in anticipation of Christ while we live after Christ's coming. We therefore no longer live in the same theological context.

- The Old Testament contains some disturbing accounts of the violent destruction of the enemies of God's people.

Perhaps it is easy to see why the Old Testament has often been neglected, except by those who have an interest in history or archaeology. Its stories tend to be treated as that – just stories, often taught in churches to children who appreciate tales of great heroes and who manage not to be troubled by the violence. Sadly the Old Testament often remains in the children's department. The Gospels, and especially the letters of Paul, tend to dominate the church adult curriculum, with the possible exception of Psalms and Proverbs. And yet, the Old Testament constitutes over three-quarters of our Bible!

THE OLD TESTAMENT IN THE EARLY CHURCH

When we turn to the beliefs and practices of the early church, however, a very different picture emerges. It is easy to forget that for many years what we call the Old Testament was the only text the early church had. It clearly was relevant to them, even though they lived at the start of a brand new era.

So, before we consider how we should approach our study of the Old Testament, it might be helpful to think this through a little more. What did the church in the New Testament do with the Scriptures?

When we look at the evidence of the New Testament, it quickly becomes clear that **the Old Testament played a central role both in evangelism and in the nurture and development of the church.**

THE OLD TESTAMENT AND EVANGELISM

Paul's evangelism to the Jews in Rome is described by Luke in these words: "From morning till evening he explained and declared to them the kingdom of God and tried to convince them about Jesus from the Law of Moses and the Prophets."[1] Luke describes Paul's teaching in Thessalonica this way: "he reasoned with them from the Scriptures, explaining and proving that the Christ had to suffer and rise from the dead."[2] The Scriptures mentioned here were, let's remind ourselves, the Old Testament Scriptures.

If it is protested here that Paul was addressing Jews and of course he would use their Scriptures, then we can point out that when it came to summing up the essence of the gospel to a church (Corinth) largely made up of Gentile converts, Paul expressed it like this: "Christ died for our sins according to the Scriptures,... he was buried... he was raised on the third day according to the Scriptures..." [3]

According to which Scriptures? According to the Old Testament Scriptures. Paul does not detail the particular Scriptures he has in mind, although no doubt such

[1] Acts 28:23

[2] Acts 17:2,3

[3] 1 Corinthians 15:3,4

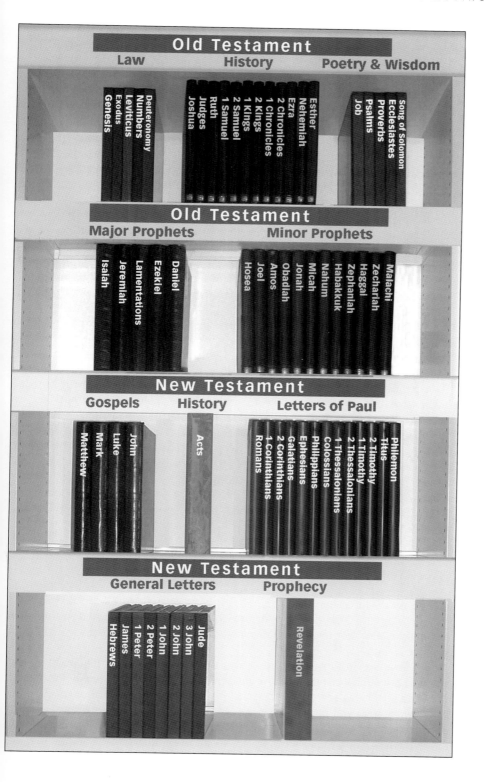

passages as Psalm 22 and Isaiah 53 were particularly in mind. Paul's letters are full of Old Testament quotations.

Why is it important that Paul is able to tell us that Christ died for our sins **according to the Scriptures?**

First, because it demonstrates that the gospel of Jesus Christ was not a human invention dreamt up by some clever philosophers in Jerusalem or Athens. Christianity is not primarily a philosophy or a moral code. It is inextricably tied to history. It did not arrive unannounced. It was "promised beforehand through his prophets in the Holy Scriptures." [4]

[4] Romans 1:1,2

Second, because it provides us with guidance on how to interpret the Cross. It is not left up to us to decide the true significance of the Cross and to reduce it, as some do, merely to an example of loving self-sacrifice which we should emulate. Both through explicit statements such as the famous "he was pierced for our transgressions... and the Lord has laid on him the iniquity of us all",[5] and through the graphic symbolism of Passover and the God-given sacrificial system, the Holy Spirit provided thought models that would enable people to see both the need for and the significance of the death of Christ. The idea of Jesus' death as a sacrifice for sin was not invented by the early church, it was carefully pictured and anticipated in the Old Testament.

[5] Isaiah 53:5,6

Third, it provides us a way of recognising the real Saviour when he comes. Many others have come and no doubt will come claiming to be the Great One, the Messiah in some form or other. But none apart from Jesus fulfils the prophesies and pictures-in-advance of the Old Testament.

It follows that while it is possible to be a believer in Christ without knowing anything of this background, fully to grasp the meaning of the gospel and to appreciate its roots in history (rather than in the fertile imagination of some 1st Century Jews) we need the Old Testament. The detail it provides in terms of illustration and symbol helps us to grasp the many aspects of the salvation that Christ has brought to us. So it is that Paul can write to Timothy about the fact that "from infancy you have known the holy Scriptures, which are able to make you wise for salvation through faith in Christ Jesus."[6] And so it was that the new believers in the town of Berea were able to "examine the Scriptures every day to see if what Paul said was true."[7]

[6] 2 Timothy 3:15

[7] Acts 17:11

THE OLD TESTAMENT AND DISCIPLESHIP

We have quoted the verse before but it bears repeating: "All Scripture is God-breathed and is useful for teaching, rebuking, correcting and training in righteousness, so that the man [and woman] of God may be thoroughly equipped for every good work."[8]

[8] 2 Timothy 3:16,17

All Scripture, in Timothy's context, was the Old Testament. It follows that if we are to be thoroughly equipped for life and service for God, we need the Old Testament.

Once again this becomes increasingly obvious when we read through the New Testament letters and observe how the writers use the Old. When Peter wants to demonstrate God's ability to rescue his people he quotes the example of Lot (2 Peter 2:7 and Genesis 19). When Paul wants to talk about spiritual gifts he quotes from the

Psalms (Ephesians 4:8 and Psalm 68:18). When John wants to talk about loving one another he quotes the negative example of Cain (1 John 3:12 and Genesis 4:8). When the writer to the Hebrews wants to explain the basis of our relationship with God through Christ he expounds Jeremiah (Hebrews 10:15-17 and Jeremiah 31:34). When James talks of the grace God gives those who remain loyal to Christ he quotes the Proverbs (James 4:6 and Proverbs 3:34).

The lessons God taught through a variety of means to his people in the Old Testament are still profitable to us. "These things happened to them as examples" writes Paul of Israel's desert wanderings, "and were written down as warnings for us, on whom the fulfilment of the ages has come." [9] Or again to the believers in Rome, "everything that was written in the past was written to teach us, so that through endurance and the encouragement of the Scriptures we might have hope." [10]

[9] 1 Corinthians 10:11

[10] Romans 15:4

What greater example could we have of the strategic, real-life importance of the Old Testament than that of the Lord Jesus himself who in the thick of his battle with Satan directly quoted from Deuteronomy?[11] If our survival in the spiritual warfare of today depended on our knowledge and understanding of Deuteronomy, I wonder how we would have done?

[11] Matthew 4:1-11

UNDERSTANDING THE OLD TESTAMENT

This should be enough to convince us, if we need convincing, of the central importance of the Old Testament, not only to our doctrine and proclamation of the Gospel, but also to Christian living and equipping for service. **How do we set about getting its message?**

Many of the principles we have already worked through in our study of Philippians will be of importance here.

- Approach each book in light of its particular literary genre – letters as letters, poetry as poetry, etc

- Consider each book as a whole

- Grasp the big picture before moving to the smaller details

- Read and interpret in the light of context

- Answer the big question: why is this book in the Bible?

- Look for the principal aspects of the gospel which are emphasised in this book

- Study what is said in this book about the divine Persons

- Discern the particular diagnosis of the human condition and God's answer(s) to it that are given in this book

- Follow the thought-flow, noting what goes with what, so that both the main and the detailed messages of the book are clear

However, there are some additional interpretive principles that will greatly help us, so we need to spend some time establishing these, and applying at least some of them to the study of one Old Testament book.

- **First,** we need to keep in mind the **historical context:** how each book fits into the flow of Old Testament history.

- **Second**, we need to think of the **theological context**: how each book fits into the bigger picture of God's unfolding revelation in the Old Testament as a whole.

- **Third,** we need to **consider the Old Testament in light of the New Testament.**

In the remainder of this unit we will consider the first two of these quite briefly. The third will need a unit of its own because there we will be considering how the New Testament itself guides us as to how to interpret and apply the Old. Finally, we will complete this short excursion into the Old Testament by seeking to apply the principles we have been learning to one book: the Book of Ruth.

HISTORICAL CONTEXT

The Books of the Old Testament were not written down in the narrowly concentrated time span as we found to be the case with the New Testament. That means that we will need to pay special attention to the changing **historical context** of each book, identifying where it comes in the flow of biblical history.

If you are relatively new to Bible study and know very little if anything of biblical history it would be very important that you build for yourself **a basic chronology of the key events.** The best way to do this is to read through the Old Testament! If you have already started to do this, as I recommended at the start of this guide, you will already have begun this task.

I am grateful to my Christian upbringing for many things, but in this area either it was lacking or I was not paying attention. There was little shape or organisation to how the Bible was taught. On any one Sunday I could hear four or five teachings, all from different parts of the Bible. While I became aware of the main characters, it was very difficult to know how it all fitted together and so any sense of progress, of the unfolding revelation, of the developing promises to be fulfilled in Christ was largely absent.

This is so important that in his introduction to the life of Christ **Matthew sets out a simple outline of the history of God's people in the Old Testament.**[12] This is a clear indication to us that in Matthew's view, the whole of the Old Testament was a preparation for the coming of Messiah. This was the 'way' [13] that God had been preparing, the road down which Messiah would eventually come.

[12] Matthew 1:1-17

[13] Matthew 3:3

Matthew's division of biblical history is very helpful. He divides it into three major periods or movements: [14]

Movement 1 **Abraham to David (1:1-6)**
Movement 2 **David to the Babylonian exile (1:6-11)**
Movement 3 **The exile to the birth of Christ (1:12-17)**

[14] I am indebted for this insight to a series of Bible studies on Matthew led by Professor David Gooding, of Queen's University, Belfast, in the early seventies.

The first eleven chapters of Genesis are in a sense the prologue, setting the scene: the Creation, the Fall, the flood and its aftermath, particularly the development of civilisation in association with Babylon. God's great purpose, to bring in the One who would crush Satan, begins in earnest (from a human perspective) with **the calling of Abraham out of Babylon.** This is the great event that sets in motion God's purpose that through Abraham and his seed all the nations of the world will be blessed.

It might be helpful to sketch in some of the major ingredients of each movement. If you know the history well, then feel free to skip to the next section (theological context).

MOVEMENT 1: ABRAHAM TO DAVID (1:1-6)
Old Testament books: Genesis to 2nd Samuel

- The prologue: Creation, the fall, the flood, the establishing of cities including Babylon.
- The call of Abraham and the **promises** made to him: to make of him a great nation; to give them a particular land; through him and his descendants to bring blessing to the world; to establish kings.
- The development of Abraham's family especially through Isaac and Jacob (renamed Israel) and his twelve sons.
- Abraham's descendants move to Egypt where one of Jacob's sons, Joseph becomes the economic saviour of Egypt and the surrounding countries.
- Exodus details how Abraham's family multiply over 400 years, but also how they become slaves in Egypt. Through Moses God delivers them and brings them through the desert to the Promised Land.
- Under the leadership of Joshua they enter and begin the conquest of the land. During this time Israel is ruled by Judges, but eventually this period of history climaxes in the enthronement of David as King, the dawn of Israel's golden age.

MOVEMENT 2: DAVID TO THE BABYLONIAN EXILE (1:6-11)
Old Testament books: 2nd Samuel, Kings, much of Chronicles, some Psalms and prophets such as Isaiah, Jeremiah, Daniel, Amos

- David establishes Jerusalem as the royal capital, and is promised a son who will build a house for God and David's royal line is to be established forever

- Solomon succeeds to the throne on David's death, builds a magnificent temple and Israel prospers at first. However Solomon compromises with idolatry and the nation begins to disintegrate. When he dies, ten tribes set up on their own becoming more and more idolatrous and eventually they are taken into captivity in Assyria.

- The remaining tribes fare better for a time, but eventually succumb to idolatry. God allows Nebuchadnezzar to sack Jerusalem, destroy the temple, take the precious temple ornaments into the temple of his own God in Babylon, and take into captivity the best and the brightest of the young men, of whom Daniel is one.

MOVEMENT 3: THE EXILE TO CHRIST (1:12–17)

Old Testament books: Daniel, Ezra, Nehemiah and the prophets of the return such as Haggai and Malachi

- Daniel concerns himself with God's promise through Jeremiah that the captivity in Babylon will not last forever and there will be a return to Jerusalem.

- This return happens in the reign of Cyrus, king of Persia – see 2 Chronicles 36:22 and Ezra 1. Under the leadership of Nehemiah the walls and gates of Jerusalem are restored, and under the leadership of Ezra the temple is rebuilt.

- However, there is no return to the Golden Age of David and Solomon – the land remains under the domination of foreign powers.

- Daniel learns that history has much bigger dimensions than the return of the captives to Jerusalem, and that God's promise of the coming of the Son of Man will still be fulfilled.

- Nothing of the history of the 400 years before the coming of the Messiah is recorded in the Old Testament. Clearly, no more words from God are required until the Word incarnate comes.

Time-lines are not easy for many of us to retain, and like me you may have struggled with history at school. Matthew's simple division should help us to sort out the major movements of Old Testament history, and give us an overall scheme into which we can fit each particular book as we study it.

As part of identifying the historical context of each book, it is also helpful to find out about the **religious, social and cultural context.** Here commentaries, or general introductions to the history of the Old Testament will be of enormous benefit, giving many insights that will be invaluable in understanding this ancient world in which God was speaking and acting.

THEOLOGICAL CONTEXT

This is where we consider **how each book fits into the bigger picture of God's revelation in the Old Testament as a whole.** God did not choose to say all he wanted to say at one time, in one book, any more than he chose to do all that he wanted to do at one point in history. Instead the Old Testament charts the course of God's unfolding revelation of his character and purposes.

As Matthew indicates, there are a number of major watershed moments in the history of God's ancient people: the calling out of Abraham, the establishing of David as king, the exile and the return. The periods marked by these key events are not just movements in history, but movements in God's revelation of himself and in the spiritual lessons he was teaching his people. As Stephen pointed out in his history lesson to an increasingly angry crowd,[15] God was not static – he kept moving on, even when the people didn't want to and opposed him at every step.

It is worthwhile to take a moment to consider some of the major spiritual lessons God was teaching his people during each of the three major movements:

Movement 1

In this movement, many of the foundational spiritual truths were first taught to the nation.

The calling of Abraham out of the idolatry of Babylon is described by Stephen as the revelation of the God of glory.[16] This is one of the biggest spiritual lessons of the Old Testament: the revelation of the glory of the one true God against the backdrop of idolatry and religious pluralism.

The promises given to Abraham make specific the promise in Genesis 3:15, and give direction and purpose to the whole of the Old Testament, and on into the New. In addition, some of the biggest spiritual truths in the Bible are taught to Abraham: justification by faith and unconditional promise. This period also includes lessons on redemption, on the need for substitutionary atonement, on holiness, and it sees the establishing of the Old Covenant based on the Ten Commandments, and the establishing of the symbolic dwelling place of God among his people. It is in this movement that the issue of Israel's inheritance in the land is first introduced, and the movement reaches its climax in the ascension of the true King to the throne.

Movement 2

In the second movement, additional promises are given concerning the royal line of David. The Temple is built and there are many lessons at the level of kingship and government, both positive and negative.

Israel's incipient tendency to idolatry surfaces again and again, ultimately leading to the exile, so that deep lessons are eventually learned by the nation regarding the fundamental and absolute importance of their faith in the one true God. The great irony is that whereas Abraham was called out of Babylon as a protest against idolatry, the people now find themselves back in Babylon as a result of their idolatry.

[15] Acts 7

[16] Acts 7:2

Movement 3

The third period witnesses the return to Jerusalem, and the rebuilding of the city and the Temple. There is a significant spiritual revival under Nehemiah and Ezra, as the nation once again seeks to get back to loyalty to the one true God and to living under the authority of his Word. At the same time there is a recognition that this rebuilding is not the final answer, and that ultimate salvation and the fulfilling of God's promises will not rest on any purely human king or political system. It is during this period that the promises of God concerning the coming Son of Man come to the fore and the movement ends in anticipation of this great event.

The relevance of this outline will become clearer when we consider the Book of Ruth (which comes towards the end of the first movement). But we have our third major principle of Old Testament interpretation still to consider: **interpreting the Old in light of the New,** and to that we must turn in the next unit.

THE OLD IN THE NEW

It is clear from what we have already seen that the **Old Testament does not stand on its own**, and was never intended to. The story is unfinished when we have read the book of Malachi, the revelation incomplete, the promises and prophecies unfulfilled. The climax and fulfilment centres on the coming of Messiah. Reading the Old Testament in light of Jesus Christ is one of the most important guiding principles to the proper interpretation and application of the Old Testament.

JESUS AND THE OLD TESTAMENT

This is how Jesus himself viewed the Old Testament. To a group of students of the Scriptures he said, "You diligently study the Scriptures because you think that by them you possess eternal life. These are the Scriptures that testify about me... If you believed Moses, you would believe me, for **he wrote about me**." [1] (Emphasis added)

While speaking to some rather despondent people who thought that his death in Jerusalem was the end of their hopes, he provided this key to unlocking the full significance of the Old Testament: "He said to them, "How foolish you are, and how slow of heart to believe all that the prophets have spoken! Did not the Christ have to suffer these things and then enter his glory?" And beginning with Moses and all the Prophets, he explained to them what was said in all the Scriptures concerning himself." [2]

Note the emphasis: **ALL** that the prophets have spoken, **ALL** the Prophets, **ALL** the Scriptures. From Genesis to Malachi there are things concerning Christ in all the Scriptures. To try to understand them solely in their own right is to miss their full significance. To understand the Old Testament, according to Jesus, we need to see what they say about him.

The Old Testament Scriptures point forward to him. The coming of Christ, and in particular his death and resurrection are the main keys to understanding fully their

[1] John 5:39, 40, 46

[2] Luke 24:25-27

combined message. As Luke puts it later in the same incident: "Then he opened their minds so they could understand the Scriptures. He told them, 'This is what is written: the Christ will suffer and rise from the dead on the third day, and repentance and forgiveness of sins will be preached in his name to all nations, beginning at Jerusalem.'" (Luke 24:45-47)

As we read the Old Testament in the light of Christ, two other major principles come into play: the principles of **continuity** and of **discontinuity.**

THE PRINCIPLE OF CONTINUITY

We have already seen that there is a strong **continuity** between Old and New Testaments. They fit together. The New heavily depends on the Old. It does not replace it. The small sample of quotations that we have used shows us some of the ways in which this dependence is expressed: illustrations from history, direct quotations of exhortations and principles, symbols and pictures, prophecy and fulfilment.

We can therefore expect major similarities between the two. For example:

- the attributes of God do not change: the God who speaks in the Old Testament is the same God who speaks in the New

- the human condition is still the same: sin is still sin, the human heart is still deceitful and sick

- the basis on which we are declared to be right before God is the same: faith not works. Both Testaments hold up Abraham as the key example of what it means to be 'justified by faith'

- the basic principle of atonement through substitutionary sacrifice runs through both Testaments

- prayer is still as vital, as is holiness, generosity, loyalty to God, hatred of idolatry in all its forms, and so on

While this is true, it is equally true that with the coming of Christ certain things change.

THE PRINCIPLE OF DISCONTINUITY

With the coming of Christ, as Stephen pointed out in his defence in Acts 7, there is a huge and irreversible leap forward in God's dealings with human beings. Let's review some of the major changes:

1. New Testament believers in Jesus Christ live under the terms of a New Covenant, predicted through Jeremiah, and now enacted by Christ through his cross and symbolised now for us by the cup of the new covenant which we take when we celebrate the Lord's Supper. That New Covenant is not a continuation of the Old, nor is it an improved version of the Old: it is different both in its nature and in its terms (Luke 22:20; Hebrews 8:6-13).

2. The Old Testament sacrificial system is fulfilled in Christ. Christ's sacrifice is not another in a long line of sacrifices. It is a sacrifice of a different order which, once offered, has entirely abolished the old system. While the Passover, or the burnt offering, provide thought models for understanding the sacrifice of Christ, we do not continue to practise animal sacrifices. Christ IS our Passover – we don't need to continue with the literal ritual. Christ IS the propitiation for our sins – we don't need to continue with the sacrifice of goats or lambs. Indeed, to continue with them would be to deny the once-for-all-time sacrifice of Christ. The fact is that the blood of lambs, bulls and goats never took away sin. They were shadows of the coming reality, they were pictures-in-advance of the atonement accomplished through the blood of Christ (see 1 Corinthians 5:7; Hebrews 10:1-18).

3. The coming of the Holy Spirit at Pentecost was not simply a step up in the Spirit's activity: this was something totally new, a fulfilment of Joel's prophecy. Rather than come upon individuals for a time, the Holy Spirit would now indwell individuals on the basis of their placing faith in Christ (Acts 2:1-21; John 14:16-18).

4. The Body of Christ is not simply a continuation of the Old Testament people of God, now opened out to include Gentiles. It is the creation of **one new man**. It has nothing to do with race or physical birth – it is a spiritual entity brought about by Christ who baptises people in the Spirit, irrespective of race, status and religious background, and gives them the same Spirit to 'drink', that is to indwell them so that all share the same life (see Ephesians 2:15; 1 Corinthians 12:12, 13, 27).

5. The New Testament 'temple' is not an improved version either of Moses' Tabernacle, or Solomon's temple. It is not a temple of literal stone, wood and gold: it is a temple made up of people, believers in Christ. There are no sacred buildings in the New Testament (see 1 Corinthians 3:16; 1 Peter 2:4,5; Ephesians 2:19-22).

6. The New Testament warfare is not a more sophisticated version of swords and spears. It is a spiritual warfare, and the weapons we use are not fleshly but spiritual. Jesus strictly forbade his followers the use of physical violence either to promote or to defend the gospel (John 18:11, 36; Ephesians 6:10-17; 1 Timothy 6:12).

7. The New Testament priesthood is not a continuation of one tribe out of twelve, or its equivalent in a Gentile context. Under the terms of the New Covenant **ALL** believers are priests (1 Peter 2:9; Revelation 5:10). While there are distinctions of gift and role in the New Testament church, there is no specialised priesthood that either has special access to God or is responsible for significant spiritual ministry. We all have access, we are all called to spiritual ministry.

The discontinuity between Old and New was not invented by the Apostles. As the early Christian teachers noted, it was **the Old Testament itself** that pointed out the need for change and prophesied its coming. For example, as we have seen, it was Jeremiah who prophesied of the coming of the New Covenant; it was Joel who prophesied the coming new age of the Spirit. Many of the Old Testament writers pointed to the inadequacy of animal sacrifices. Psalm 110 points out that David's Lord was to be a High Priest for ever, not the temporary, mortal priesthood that Israel had under the Old Covenant.

The dangers of seeing the New Testament merely as a continuation of the old are many when it comes to the interpretation and application of the Old Testament. Each of the following applications in the history of the church is arguably the result of this mistake:

- Encouraging Christians to take up arms either to defend or to promote the gospel

- Creating holy buildings which have no-go areas where only a specialised priesthood can enter

- Confining significant spiritual ministry to a specialised priesthood or clergy

- Modelling church leadership structures on the leadership structures of Israel, and modelling leadership style on the great political as well as spiritual leaders of Israel, such as Moses or David

- Tying the gospel to a particular piece of real estate, or to a particular political viewpoint

And so we could continue. The point for our purposes is that there is both **continuity** and **discontinuity** between Old and New Testaments. We believers today live in a very different stage of God's activity than did Abraham, or Moses, or Ruth, or Solomon.

KEY QUESTIONS

As we seek to learn lessons from the Old Testament we must keep this in mind. We need to ask:

- what did this passage/incident/law/principle mean, and how did it apply, to its original audience?

- what is the continuity between their situation and ours? What key underlying principles still apply to us today?

- what is the discontinuity between their situation and ours? What difference is there for us who now live under the terms of the New Covenant?

RELEVANCE

This principle of discontinuity is sometimes overlooked, or downplayed, with serious results. At the same time it can also be overplayed, with the serious result that we could come to feel that large parts of the Old Testament are no longer relevant for us, now that Christ has come.

For example, what are we to make of the genealogies and lists in Numbers, the seemingly endless accounts of warfare in Judges, the long (and boring?) chapters of Exodus devoted to building instructions for the Tabernacle, the intricate and gory details of the sacrifices in Leviticus? How can these things be relevant for us? After all, doesn't the New Testament warn us about people who are overly interested in genealogies? And aren't we forbidden to use violence in the cause of Christ? And haven't we already seen that the Old Testament sacrifices are obsolete according to Hebrews? (Some down through the history of the church have gone as far as to claim that the entire Old Testament is irrelevant to Christians!)

Once again, we need to be reminded of what we have said in these units concerning how the New Testament writers, the early church in general, and Christ himself treated the Old Testament. It is very far from irrelevant. All Scripture is profitable.

In what way is it profitable? How should we interpret, for example, some of these remote and obsolete institutions and practices in a way that is profitable for us today, without allowing imagination to run away with us on one hand, or excessive caution to prevent us seeing the application to us on the other?

THE PRINCIPLE OF BEING GUIDED BY THE NEW TESTAMENT WRITERS

Not only do we need to read the Old Testament in light of the coming of Christ, but also we should **follow the interpretive leads given to us by the New Testament writers** in how they understand, use and apply the Old Testament.

Frequently, for example, as the New Testament writers seek to illustrate a key point, they refer to an Old Testament character. Why not check some of these out for yourself and discover the great benefit it is in the interpretation of Old Testament stories?

Example 1: Cain

- Step 1: read the story from Genesis 4
- Step 2: read the New Testament commentaries: Hebrews 11:4, 1 John 3:12 and Jude 1:11
- Step 3: note down the key insights provided by these authors for understanding and applying the story of Cain

Example 2: Esau:

- Step 1: read the story from Genesis 27:1-40
- Step 2: read the New Testament commentary: Hebrews 12:16
- Step 3: note down the key insights provided by the author of Hebrews for understanding and applying this story

Example 3: Noah

- Step 1: read the story from Genesis 6:9 to Genesis 9:17
- Step 2: use a concordance to find all the references to Noah or to the flood in the New Testament
- Step 3: list each occurrence and then for each write down the main teaching point from how the New Testament teachers, including in this case Christ himself, use the story. (If you do not have a concordance – here are a few NT references: Luke 17:26; Hebrews 11:7; 2 Peter 3:6).

In each of these cases the New Testament writers provide us with invaluable pointers as to how to interpret and to apply the Old Testament stories.

In addition, you may have noted that the New Testament authors often focus on different aspects of the same Old Testament character or event. Consider again the example of Cain. In Hebrews the focus is on the sacrifice Cain made in contrast to that of Abel. John, in the context of an exhortation to believers to love one another, highlights the fact that Cain murdered his brother. Jude is speaking of godless people who reject authority and pollute all around them, saying that they have gone in **'the way of Cain'.** This is not simply a focus on Cain's approach to sacrifice, but on the aftermath, on his whole way of going in life. Genesis 4 describes in some detail what this 'way' is: to go 'in the way of Cain' is to defy God and to become an aimless fugitive on earth.

HELP FROM THE OLD TESTAMENT

Some Old Testament writers themselves also help us here. In many cases the later books of the Old Testament provide their own spiritual commentary on characters, incidents and institutions from the earlier books, and when they do, this is a great advantage to us as we seek the correct interpretation and application of the lessons of their lives.

For example, in the book of Nehemiah, lessons from the final and disastrous period of Solomon's life are applied by Nehemiah to the people of his day.[3] The Book of Ruth contains many references to major characters from earlier history, such as Rachel and Leah.[4] These references give us certain pointers to the significance of Ruth's story.

The Psalms frequently comment on major events in God's dealings with Israel – for example Psalm 135 comments on the exodus and the giving of the land to Israel as a heritage. Psalm 110 indicates that there is an eternal priestly order in the line of Melchizedek, a character who only appears in Genesis 14, and then only briefly.

[3] Nehemiah 13:26,27

[4] Ruth 4:11

Jeremiah, as we have already seen, comments on the inadequacy of the Old Covenant system and on the need for a new covenant.[5] Daniel comments on Jeremiah's prophecy concerning the return.[6] In Hosea, Judah's disloyalty is compared to Adam's,[7] and Ephraim's depravity is compared to the horrific events of Gibeah as recounted in Judges 19. Zechariah points to some of the deeper spiritual significance of the Lampstand in the Tabernacle/Temple.[8] In addition, therefore, to checking out references in the New Testament to the passages we are studying, we will often find helpful pointers in the Old.

[5] Jeremiah 31:31-34
[6] Daniel 9:2
[7] Hosea 6:7

[8] Zechariah 4:1-6

CONCLUSION

My point in this section is not to introduce all the different ways in which the New Testament makes use of the Old, but to establish the principle that **in our interpretation and application of the Old Testament we should allow ourselves, wherever possible, to be guided by the writers of the New Testament.**

16 PICTURES IN ADVANCE

(Because of the more technical nature of this Chapter you may wish simply to read the summary of principles of Old Testament interpretation and then continue to Unit 17 where we consider the Old Testament Book of Ruth.)

It is clear from the New Testament writers that in addition to providing illustrations and lessons from history, much of the Old Testament contains God-designed **pictures-in-advance** of the person and achievement of the Lord Jesus Christ. This is particularly true of the ritual, festivals, sacrificial system and priesthood established under the Old Covenant.

You may have already discovered that long chapters of Exodus are devoted to detail of the design of the Tabernacle, the portable temple the Children of Israel carried with them on their journey from Egypt to the Promised Land. On the principle that all Scripture is profitable, we might struggle to grasp where precisely the profitability for us lies in such details. Are these chapters profitable simply for the historical and architectural detail they give, and for the insights they give into the Old Covenant procedures for worship? Or have they any further meaning other than that significance they carried for their original audience?

The author of Hebrews finds them very significant, not just for ancient Israel but also for the church. In Chapter 9 he reminds the readers of the basic design of the Tabernacle and arrangement of furniture. Intriguingly he comments "we cannot discuss these things in detail now",[1] implying, surely, that given a different context and different purpose for writing he could indeed discuss them in detail. However, he focuses our attention on one of the details – the two compartment arrangement of the Tabernacle: its division into "outer room" and "inner room." [2]

The significance of this is clear: while this two compartment arrangement was in place, "The Holy Spirit was showing by this that the way into the Most Holy Place had not yet been disclosed."[3] The arrangement was not accidental, nor was it designed by a human architect. It was a Holy Spirit designed illustration that the way

[1] Hebrews 9:5

[2] Hebrews 9:6, 7

[3] Hebrews 9:8

into God's presence could not depend on animal sacrifices, for such sacrifices "were not able to clear the conscience of the worshipper."[4] The arrangement pointed to the inadequacy of the sacrificial system: it had no final solution to the problem of human guilt.

[4] Hebrews 9:9, 10

The illustration was not just for Israel. "This is an illustration for the present time", says the writer, and goes on to demonstrate how this God-given arrangement pointed forward to the coming of the final solution through the death of Christ, by which our consciences are cleansed from dead works so that we can freely serve the living God.[5] There is no division, no veil now to separate us from the throne of God – we can come to it boldly, with confidence, any time we wish and be sure of welcome. The Old Testament arrangement was a picture-in-advance of the supreme achievement of the death of Christ.

[5] Hebrews 9:14

Once again the New Testament has come to our help in making sense of a major part of the Old Testament.

AVOIDING EXTREMES

So far so good. However, some Christian theologians and preachers, stimulated by this example, have tried to find such pictures-in-advance in almost every major detail of the Old Testament (and in a few minor details). Their extremes have led to a widespread and negative reaction in many quarters to this approach to the interpretation of the Old Testament.

Many suggest that nothing in the Old Testament should be regarded as a picture-in-advance of anything, unless explicitly warranted by the New Testament.[6] In all other cases, resorting to typological interpretation brings us into a realm where there are no controls, everything is subjective and arbitrary. In addition, this fanciful approach to interpretation usually ends up with the original and primary meaning of the Old Testament text being either obscured or completely obliterated.

[6] The theological term for what I have called a picture-in-advance is a type, defined by Robertson McQuilkin as a 'prophetic symbol' – see McQuilkin, op cit, p 259. A type is an object, or institution or person that in someway – not necessarily in every detail – foreshadows the future. Paul tells us that Adam is a type (NIV pattern) of "the one to come", that is, Christ (Romans 5:14). The Greek word sometimes translated **type** is also used in the NT in the sense of example (Philippians 3:17; 1 Corinthians 10:6, 11).

This negative reaction is understandable and yet it is not without its own dangers and extremes. It runs the risk of making the Old Testament very one-dimensional. And it runs the risk that people will avoid large portions of the Old Testament (and the New Testament) altogether, through fear of getting things wrong, thus robbing themselves and others of some of the richness and variety of Scripture.

To help us avoid such extremes, it might be useful to consider two worked examples where I seek to interpret significant portions of the Old Testament, without allowing my imagination to run away with me. It is up to you to decide whether or not I have succeeded!

WORKED EXAMPLE 1 – PASSOVER

Let's take the Passover as an example. Paul tells the Corinthians that **"Christ our Passover has been sacrificed..."** [7], associating the death of Christ with the Old Testament event and festival.

[7] 1 Corinthians 5:7

Passover was established by God through Moses in Exodus 12. It had to do with the deliverance of God's people, and in particular the first-born, not only from their bondage as slaves in Egypt by breaking Pharaoh's hold on them, but also from the wrath of God against sin.

At the heart of Passover was the instruction to select an unblemished lamb, to kill it without breaking any of its bones, and to paint the blood of the sacrificed lamb on the door posts and lintel of each home. Paul clearly saw in the sacrifice of the Passover lamb to deliver the firstborn in Israel from the judgement of God **a picture-in-advance** of what Jesus would accomplish on the cross as a sacrifice to deliver us from God's wrath.

This is not at all an arbitrary connection, a strained analogy which Paul claims to have found in Old Testament history, but which was never intended by God. Rather, this was God's way of teaching his people concerning the seriousness and costliness of sin, and the reality of God's judgement, and doing it in such a way that would help prepare future generations for understanding the significance of the death of his Son. When God designed the Passover, he already had in mind the coming of the Son to give himself as the Lamb of God for the sins of the world.

Christ's death was deliberately staged by God at Passover so that we would not miss the connection. John points out in his description of the crucifixion that Jesus' legs were not broken by the soldiers. "These things happened so that the Scripture would be fulfilled: 'not one of his bones will be broken...'" [8] When John the Baptist introduced Jesus to the world he was able to say, "Look, the Lamb of God who takes away the sin of the world"[9], and know that the people had a category in their thinking to enable them to understand what he was referring to.

The Passover, therefore, was a divinely inspired picture-in-advance and thought-model of the sacrifice of Christ for the sins of the world. This does not change the historic significance and impact of the original Passover: it was the means of redemption for God's people at the time.

This is, perhaps, one of the clearer and more obvious examples of an Old Testament institution which has major significance for the New.

[8] John 19:33-36

[9] John 1:29

WORKED EXAMPLE 2: THE HIGH PRIEST

Exodus Chapters 28 and 29, together with Chapter 39, are devoted to **the institution of the priesthood** in Israel, and in particular of Aaron the High Priest. Two of the chapters are largely taken up with how he was to be dressed when he went into the sanctuary to minister before God; the third chapter is focussed on the consecration of the priests.

Take a few moments to read the description - at least **28:1-43**.

Over the next few pages I am going to set out some suggestions as to how we could go about interpreting the main elements of these passages in Exodus. There are two core questions:

- what did this arrangement mean for the people at the time?
- what does it mean for us today (if anything)?

And as we work out what it might mean for us today, there are three core principles:

- the principle of continuity
- the principle of discontinuity
- the principle of being guided and controlled by the New Testament writers themselves

What did this arrangement mean for people at the time?

Read 28:1-43 again and note down
- statements that imply purpose or significance
- repeated ideas

What did you find? (NB – please write down your own observations before you read on!)

Observations:

Here are some of mine:

- repetition of **"to minister as priest(s) to me"** – three times in opening verses, and also verse 41

- the garments were **"for glory and for beauty"** (2, 40)

- the emphasis on the names of the sons of Israel engraved on precious stones

- the repetition of **"before the Lord"** (12, 29, 30, 35, 38)

- the repetition of the idea of carrying the names on the shoulders and over the heart (12, 29, 30)

- the focus on the ephod and the breastplate and the importance of the two not coming loose from each other

- the emphasis on holiness (2, 4, 29, 35, 36, 43)

- **"SO THAT he will not die"** (35)

- **"SO THAT they may be accepted"** (38)

- **"SO THAT they do not incur guilt"** (43)

On the basis of these simple observations, in particular on how the passage itself comments on the purpose or significance of the details, we could set out at least three of the basic lessons for **the people at the time:**

- God desired a genuine relationship with his people. He provided a way for connection so that people could come to know him, stand before him and speak with him.

- At the same time, there was still a distance: the 'ordinary' people were not at liberty to join the priest in the Holy Place, and even the priest could not come into that place any way he liked. This emphasised both the holiness of God and the sinfulness of man.

- Yet, the people's names were being brought before the Lord every time the breastplate was worn in his presence. The priest literally carried their names on his shoulders and over his heart as he ministered to the Lord. This, together with the fact that the names were engraved on precious stones, was clear indication to all of how valuable they were in God's sight.

These were important spiritual truths for that time. What about the **lessons and applications for us today?**

If we think about this in terms of the principle of **continuity** we could say the following:

- the insights into the heart of God towards us are still very valid and important: his desire for relationship with us, his invitation to us to come to him and his willingness to hear us, these are still the same

- in addition, God is still holy: the illustration provided by this Old Testament text gives us a visual way of thinking about his holiness

- the value of the individual, and the importance of prayer for people by name are surely the same

Let's try to take continuity a step further with the following 'applications' for our time:

- ordinary Christians do not have the highest level of access to God so therefore we need to appoint a High Priest to represent us before God

- we need to ensure that our appointed High Priest has special clothes in order properly to represent us before God

- his clothing should in some way carry the names of the people he represents

- from the wider context in Exodus it is clear we need also to have a specially consecrated building in which he can operate, together with the special robes, a golden altar and burning incense so that it is properly spiritual

I suspect that many of us will be uncomfortable with some, if not all, of these applications! Perhaps our discomfort is simply a matter of personal taste, or a hunch that somehow things are different these days, or the pragmatic belief that this approach would not work in our modern environment. But personal taste, hunches and pragmatism are not the safest principles of interpretation!

Let's instead apply our principle of **discontinuity** based on the teaching of the New Testament.

COPIES AND SHADOWS

The New Testament is extremely helpful to us on the issue of the High Priest because it deals with it specifically and at some length, especially in the book of Hebrews. So we can be guided in our interpretation and application of this part of Old Testament Scripture not just by the general teaching of the New, but also by the specific and detailed references.

The general teaching of Hebrews is that the Law with its sacrifices and rituals "is only a shadow of the good things to come, not the realities themselves." (Hebrews 10:1) The priests still operating in Jerusalem at the time of writing "serve at a sanctuary that is a copy and shadow of heavenly things." (Hebrews 8:5)

Note the terms: **copy** and **shadow:**

- A **copy** in the sense that items of furniture used in the sanctuary such as the Altar of Sacrifice and the Lampstand, together with the rituals associated with them, reflected eternal truths, making them much more concrete and real to ordinary folks - much in the same way as we might teach our children abstract concepts of value through using toy money.

- At the same time they were still only **shadows** of the coming good things, not the realities themselves. The shadows point forward – they **foreshadow** the good things to come in Christ.

How does this help us in our interpretation of the passage in Exodus 28 concerning the High Priest, and in our application of its truth to our lives today? Hebrews spells it out for us.

First, we do **not** need to elect within our Christian communities a High Priest to intercede for us with God, for God has already appointed one: Jesus Christ our Lord. Indeed the main point of Hebrews (Chapter 8:1) is that **we have a High Priest.**

Second, Christ is not simply another priest in a long line of priests. He belongs to a different order of priesthood altogether, in fulfilment of Psalm 110:4 "You are a priest forever after the order of Melchizedek." He is eternal.

Third, Christ is infinitely superior to the Old Testament priesthood – an important point, especially for those who, in the time Hebrews was written, were strongly tempted to go back to the more tangible and sensual ceremonial still taking place in the Temple.

Christ's superiority is spelled out by the author of Hebrews in a number of ways. Here are some of them:

- One of the problems with the Old Testament High Priest was that he did not continue – no sooner had you got to know him than he died, and his replacement died. Christ, by contrast, lives in the power of an endless life! (Hebrews 7:23-25)

- Another of the problems under the old system was that however spiritual the High Priests were, they were still sinners and powerless to do anything about either their sin or the sins of the people. They even had to offer a special sacrifice for themselves before they could offer a sacrifice for the people. However, our High Priest, Christ, is sinless and was able to offer a perfect sacrifice which has dealt with the problem of our guilt once for all time (Hebrews 7:26-28).

We notice what is happening here. The writer is taking some of the details concerning the Old Testament High Priests and using them, both by means of similarities and, in particular, of contrasts, to point out the superiority and magnificence of Jesus as High Priest.

This is important, for, without these specific Old Testament details, we might easily have missed these aspects of Christ as High Priest.

In this respect, Old Testament symbolism operates similarly to a tourist brochure we might read in preparation for travel. The brochure is not the real thing, of course, but it helps us to **recognise the real thing when we see it.** (There is no point in thinking that we have arrived in Paris, if in fact we have come to Madrid!) In addition, the brochure points to **details of the reality that we might otherwise have missed.** (The pictures and details of Paris will help us make the most of it when we arrive.)

The implications of this interpretation are obvious for the Hebrews and for ourselves. If we have Jesus as our High Priest, why would we need or want anyone else? If Christ has raised us all to the status of priest, why would we dress one of us up as our special representative? And since the temple is now made up of living stones, why would we go back to dead lumps of granite and marble and call this the dwelling place of God?

THE STONES AND THE NAMES

What of the details given in Exodus 28 concerning the **precious stones** and the **engraved names?** Is there additional significance to be found here, or should we simply focus on the main lessons above and be very wary of an overheated imagination?

If we ask what it meant to the Old Testament people, the answer is obvious: the High Priest carried the names of the people (represented by the names of the twelve tribes) as he ministered before the Lord, so that, for example, when he prayed at the Altar of Incense he literally carried on his person the names of the people for whom he was making intercession.

Is there any similarity or contrast here with what Christ does for us as High Priest? What exactly does he do for us as our High Priest? We have a number of examples of Christ in prayer for his disciples (and indeed for us[10]). One of the most striking is where Luke gives us this detail from the night of Christ's betrayal: "Simon, Simon, Satan has asked to sift you as wheat. But I have prayed for you, Simon, that your faith may not fail." (Luke 22:31,32) Here is an example of how, at a much higher level than anything the Old Testament High Priest could do, Christ acts as our High Priest, praying for his people by name.

Why do we need Christ to pray for us? From the context it is clear that Peter was facing the greatest test of his life. Instead of leaving him to face it on his own, the Son of God himself prayed for Peter. And we note **what he prayed for**: that his **faith** would not fail. Everything else failed as Peter swore that he was not one of Christ's followers. But deep down underneath Peter never ceased to be a believer. And as we consider this, perhaps we will get a much greater insight into what Christ as our High Priest is doing for us still, and it may cause us to pause and worship.

What about the specific detail that the High Priest was literally carrying the names of the people on his shoulders and across his chest?

If we consider again what this arrangement would have meant to the people at the time, the symbolism is actually very clear. As in many cultures, the Jews were in the habit of using parts of the body to express aspects of human psychology and emotional states – in much the same way as we might talk of having no stomach for a fight, shouldering responsibility, having a head for heights, or having a heart for the poor.

The language is highly effective in the context of the role of a High Priest. He literally shouldered the names of the people, as well as having them over his heart. To

[10] John 17:20

143

be an effective High Priest was to have compassion on the people and seek to share their burdens. Taking this by analogy, would it be beyond the limits of good exegesis to say that these attributes are perfectly displayed in Christ? Perhaps Hebrews itself indicates as much when we read, "We do not have a High Priest who is unable to sympathise with our weaknesses..."[11] and again, "he is able to help those who are being tempted." [12]

[11] Hebrews 4:15

[12] Hebrews 2:18

If that is too big a stretch for you, so be it! I won't go before a firing squad over this interpretation. However, it does not seem to me to be beyond the bounds of possibility. It is not arbitrary in that it is consistent with the context and the original teaching, and it is a wonderful illustration. In any case, by saying this we would not be teaching anything that is not clear from elsewhere in the New Testament. Having the visual picture, however, is a lot more fun, especially for those of us who tend to think in pictures!

GOD SPEAKS IN PICTURES-PLUS-WORDS

And this is a serious point. God by definition is the greatest and wisest teacher in the universe. He has chosen to communicate with us not just through words but through pictures-plus-words.

- Not just in pictures because a picture without words is open to all kinds of interpretation and personal speculation.

- Not just in words, for God knows how we think and knows the need most of us have for visual aids.

Allowing ourselves to be guided by how the New Testament writers themselves use the Old Testament will help us to avoid unacceptable excesses in the understanding and application of Scripture.

SUMMARY

In these last three units I have sought to condense some of the key principles we will need to apply when it comes to interpreting the Old Testament. And you have been mostly passive! That is about to change, for what will help to root what we have discussed in reality will be to apply some of these principles to the study of one of the Old Testament books. And that is what is in store for us in the next Unit.

But let's end with a summary of some of the key principles:

- **Read each book in light of its context**
  * What is the historical context of the book – where does it fit into the flow of Old Testament history?
  * What is the social/cultural context – what background information might we need to know to understand the text better?
  * What is the theological context of each book: where does it fit into the flow of God's revelation and redemptive activity?

- **Identify the main teachings of the book for its original audience**
  - * What moral and spiritual lessons were they being taught in their context?
  - * How do later Old Testament books interpret key events (if they do)?

- **Identify the main teachings of the book for us today,** being guided by the New Testament
  - * Note the **continuity** between the Old and the New – what lessons apply to us unchanged?
  - * Note the **discontinuity** between the Old and the New – what contrasts are there between the specific Old Testament situation and our context under the New Covenant?
  - * Are there specific references to and usages of this book or passage or character or concept in the New Testament so that we can be guided in our interpretation and application?
  - * Does the Old Testament itself help us here in commenting on earlier events, people or institutions?
  - * Ensure that our application of the Old Testament is in harmony with what is explicitly taught in the New.

17 BOOK OF RUTH: READING AN OLD TESTAMENT BOOK

Our purpose in this Chapter is to seek to apply some of the key principles we have been learning to a particular Old Testament book. In keeping with our choice of a short New Testament book, let's consider a short Old Testament book: the Book of Ruth.[1]

Please note: what follows can be little more than an introduction to the study of the book, otherwise another entire study guide would be required! In addition, our study will be further limited by the particular genre of the Book of Ruth itself.

[1] All quotations from Ruth are taken from the New American Standard Bible

LITERARY GENRE

By now we have been reminded on several occasions that it is important to approach each particular literary genre in the way appropriate to it – letters as letters, poetry as poetry, and so on. What kind of book is Ruth?

The Book of Ruth is a narrative, a story.

By calling it a **story** we don't of course imply that it is fiction, possibly a made-up folk-tale to make some moral or spiritual point. Some scholars regard it as such but in the New Testament Matthew includes both Ruth and Boaz in his genealogy of Messiah,[2] and the book itself appears to insist on its historicity, including exact detail of family and genealogy, in addition to historical and geographical context. It historicity is underlined by the inclusion, at the end of the book, of a genealogy which links the content and action of this book to the much larger story of God's activity i history and the bringing into the world of Israel's greatest king, David.

[2] Matthew 1:5

My approach, therefore, is that the Book of Ruth is an account of an actual even that took place in ancient times. It is **also** a wonderful story. The approach of the historian as he arranges his material, and the artist who does the same, are no necessarily opposite. Even historians do not record everything, and what they d record is not recorded merely because it happened, but because it has particular significance in terms of the purpose of the work.[3]

[3] For a fuller discussion of this, see David Gooding, According to Luke, IVP, 1987, pp 10-16, 358-359

TAKE UP AND READ

Our first task is the same as what it was with Philippians: **read the book as a whole,** so that before we examine the individual elements we grasp **the movement of the story.**

Why not take a few moments now to read it? It has only four chapters and can be read quite easily at a sitting. (If you are not sure where to find it in the Old Testament, look up the table of contents that you probably have at the front of your edition of the Bible. Ruth comes between the two much longer books of Judges and 1 Samuel, and is therefore quite easy to miss.)

What were your first impressions?

I suspect you found it even easier to read than Philippians. What a wonderful and moving story! The main characters are strong, the situation is gripping, the story moves along rapidly and the denouement is satisfying. In addition, the remarkable amount of dialogue – over half the text – gives the work quite a modern feel.

THE STORY LINE

In some ways it is easier to map and retain the contents of Ruth because there is a strong story line which we can follow. As it is always useful to do with the narrative books of the Bible, I suggest that you take time now to set out a simple outline of the story, following the chapter designations.

Chapter 1

Chapter 2

Chapter 3

Chapter 4

Your outline might look like this:

Chapter 1

1-5   The move to Moab: famine in the days of the judges - Elimelech moves with his family to Moab, where the men in the family died leaving Naomi and her two daughters-in-law.

6-22   The return to Bethlehem: news of God's provision of food inspires Naomi to return to the land of Judah. Naomi pleads with the girls to stay behind as she sees no future for the family - life is bitter and the Lord is against her. Ruth pledges loyalty to her and to her God. Naomi is recognised at Bethlehem but suggests a name change to Mara because her life is 'bitter'.

Chapter 2

1-23   Ruth working in Boaz' field. Introduction to Boaz, Naomi's relative. Ruth finds herself gleaning in his field – Boaz notices her, inquires about her identity and shows her particular kindness. Naomi recognises God's hand of kindness in this and calls Boaz a kinsman redeemer.

Chapter 3

1-18   At Naomi's suggestion, Ruth progresses her relationship with Boaz. Boaz determines to do all he can to redeem the family, and provides additional food for them.

Chapter 4

1-17   Boaz raises the issue of redemption with another kinsman redeemer who is first in line. He is prepared to redeem the land, but not when he realises he would have to take the widow, Naomi, in order to preserve the family name with the property. That clears the way for Boaz who formally redeems the property and Ruth to be his wife so that the family name will be preserved with the property. Ruth has a son, but it is expressed by the women that Naomi has a son. He is called Obed, the grandfather of David.

18-22   The family line of Perez, through Boaz to David.

This will help establish the story line in our minds. However, it is not quite the same as our 'Map of Contents,' which needs to include **more specific linguistic detail** and less comment.

Here is an example of what I mean for the first chapter. (I am using the language of the NASB rather than the NIV.)

MAP OF CONTENTS

Setting it out this way will enable us to appreciate how key themes and emphases come through the language used. Note, for example, the importance of names, of carrying on the family name through sons, the repetition of the verb return, the contrast between the famine at the start of the chapter and the harvest at the end.

THE BIG QUESTION

Does the author tell us why he (or she) is writing? (Some have the view that the strong focus of this story on women indicates that the author was a woman, but the general opinion is that this is most unlikely.)

In common with most narratives, there is no direct statement of authorial intention. Unlike Philippians the author of Ruth remains unnamed and generally quite inaccessible. There is no overt authorial intervention of the type: "I am writing this so that you will know..." This is not a letter written to a New Testament church instructing it concerning its beliefs and practices. This is a story.

This does not mean, however, either that there is no author or that we will be given no clues as to what the message of Ruth might be. As with all good stories, the way in which the story is told will guide us.

Ruth is a carefully constructed narrative. There is an economy of information, nothing is extraneous, everything fits into a harmonious whole. As with all good literature, we must approach it with the assumption that the details we are given are deliberately selected in order to do more than record an event simply because it happened, and all the more so as we are dealing with a divinely inspired account. The book has not just a story but a message.

With their strong storytelling traditions, ancient audiences were quite adept at reading and interpreting a story, in the same way that modern Western cinema audiences are likewise quite sophisticated in picking up the message of a film from the hints and guides provided by the director, however subtle they may be. Although we do not know the author of Ruth, we meet him, hear him and are guided by him through the narrative. We need to listen to the text.

How do we do that?

Some of the questions we have already applied to Philippians we can apply here. We need, for example, to look for **repeated words and concepts** which might well constitute central themes. We can look at the **particular attributes and activities of God** that are highlighted in the story. We can look at whether the **issue of salvation** is raised in any form. We can look at the **biographical details** given with regard to the main characters. We can indeed make a **diagnosis** of sorts, answering such questions as: what were the social, historical and economic conditions at the time? What were the spiritual conditions? What particular aspects of the human condition are highlighted in this story? We can use our **key-in-the-front-door** principle, and we will certainly be looking to discover the **thought-flow.**

In addition, because this is a narrative, not an apostolic teaching, there will be much more in the way of **literary device** which we need to recognise. Here are some of the things we should look for:

- what is the central action of the story?

- how does the story begin, how does it end, and how does it move from the beginning to the end?

- is there evidence that the author has structured the book so that events complement or balance each other?

- how does the author use the juxtaposition of two or more events to express his viewpoint?

- does the author use any of his characters, or any other device, to guide us towards the true significance of the story?

Much of the hard and detailed work will have to be left to you! What I want to do is simply to demonstrate how some of our questions and principles apply, and to begin to answer the question as to the relevance of the Book of Ruth, not just for its own time but for today.

READING RUTH IN ITS CONTEXT

The first principle from our summary is to **read Ruth in light of its context.** What is the **HISTORICAL CONTEXT** of the book? Where does it fit into the flow of Old Testament history?

The book itself tells us: it is set in **the time of the Judges.** Most commentators think it was set in the later period of the Judges, both from the genealogy given and the conditions of famine and difficulty that are referred to. Be that as it may, we are towards the end of Matthew's first movement. Ruth provides a bridge between the time of the Judges and the coming of King David.

What is the **CULTURAL CONTEXT**? What background information might we need to know to understand the text better?

It will certainly help us to read up a little on the time of the Judges and the conditions that prevailed particularly towards the end of this period. In addition, we should find out what we can about **Moab**, both culturally and spiritually. Where did Moab come from? What characterises Moab and Moabites in the Old Testament? How does God view Moab, particularly through the voice of the prophets? (A concordance will be invaluable here.)

There are also certain **legal institutions** in Israel that have a major bearing on the storyline of the Book of Ruth. Marriage customs come to the fore very early through what might sound to us the rather strange words of Naomi to her daughters-in-law: "Have I yet sons in my womb, that they may be your husbands?" [4] We should find out what we can about **levirate marriage.** And in connection with this, we would also need to research the regulations regarding the **kinsman redeemer,** which are probably foreign to our own culture. (A Bible dictionary or commentary will help here. You can also read the key Old Testament passages: Deuteronomy 25:5-10; Leviticus 25.)

What of the **THEOLOGICAL CONTEXT** of Ruth? Where does it fit into the flow of God's revelation and redemptive activity?

This is an end of **Movement 1** story. God's people are in the Promised Land, in their inheritance. However, as the book opens, Elimelech is struggling to make a go of his inheritance and decides to move out of the Promised Land and into Moab, with disastrous consequences. A major part of the story is about how the family through Naomi, Ruth and Boaz are restored to their inheritance. This raises all kinds of theological questions: about the provision and faithfulness of God; about the purposes of God for his people; about suffering; about restoration and how it is achieved.

[4] Ruth 1:11. See also verses 12 and 13.

THE MEANING OF RUTH FOR ITS TIME

The next key task is to seek to **identify the main teachings of this short book for its original audience.** What moral and spiritual lessons were they being taught in their context?

DIAGNOSIS

Let's begin with a diagnosis. There is a famine in the Promised Land. More specifically there is famine in Bethlehem. Bethlehem means 'the house of bread'. Elimelech decides to abandon ship with his family. As the story goes on to reveal, not everyone did. There is a strong implication that things were not as bad as Elimelech made out, and that the decision to leave Bethlehem was questionable, even on practical grounds. It was clearly questionable on the more important grounds of his trust in and loyalty towards God. To give up on God's purposes for his inheritance in the land, and to go out of the land, to Moab – a nation that had opposed God's purposes for Israel as they were travelling towards the Promised Land – was a very serious indication of his own spiritual condition.

In a different context Abraham did a similar thing, and of course Jacob went down into Egypt with God's permission, so perhaps we should go easy on Elimelech. Yet, on the face of it, there is a statement of failure here. This was the **Promised Land**, not any old country that they had happened to find themselves in. Each family had been given an inheritance in the Land, and they saw this as God-given. Why then did they leave it? Could they not take the famine as from the hand of God and trust him? Others did, like Boaz, and managed to make a go of it. But he didn't, and then he died and his sons died, and the whole thing seemed to be ending in total ruin.

Our diagnosis should also take account of Naomi. She describes herself as **empty** and **bitter**. She believes that the hand of the Lord is against her. She is bereft of both husband and sons. There is massive personal famine and suffering. Yet the story shows how she is restored not just to the inheritance, but to a hope-filled future through the birth of her grandson, in turn the grandfather of David. The movement of the story is, therefore, from bitterness to joy, from emptiness to fullness, from famine to harvest, from going against the purposes of God and questioning his goodness, to recognising his activity and kindness.

REPETITION OF KEY WORDS AND CONCEPTS

The importance of names recurs in a number of ways. The maintenance of the family name is one of the key driving forces of the plot: "in order to maintain the name of the dead with his property, so that his name will not disappear from among his family or from the town records." [5]

[5] Ruth 4:10 (NIV)

The significance of individual names is underscored in the book by Naomi herself. Her name means **pleasant** and yet she asks the women instead to call her **Mara**, which means **bitter**, stating that God has dealt bitterly with her.

There is strong emphasis, as we have seen, in the opening chapter on the concept of **returning**, which, in addition to the geographical reality of returning to Bethlehem, may well carry metaphorical implications in terms of the return to God himself. The decision by Orpah is certainly seen as not only a return to her people, but a return to her gods; while Ruth consciously expresses her decision to return with Naomi to Bethlehem as a personal commitment not just to her, but to her people and to her God.

The concept of redemption occurs frequently in Ruth – 23 times in all, a quarter of all occurrences in the Old Testament. The concept of **kindness** or **loyalty**, is important to the action of the book for it is mentioned at three key junctures: 1:8 where Naomi desires that the Lord will reward the loyalty of the daughters-in-law in kind; 2:20 where Naomi recognises the loyalty of the Lord (or is it Boaz?) to her, and in 3:10 where Boaz desires that Ruth should be blessed by the Lord for showing loyalty to him, even though he is not the young man she might naturally have desired to have as a husband.

ATTRIBUTES AND ACTIVITIES OF GOD

We see God first through Naomi's eyes. She believes in Chapter 1 that the hand of the Lord is against her, that the Almighty has dealt very bitterly with her, that he has afflicted her. At the same time she recognises that the Lord has brought her back.[6] She probably means this in a literal, geographical sense in Chapter 1. And yet even there it is more than geography. She recognises the hand of God behind her return. The positive actions of Ruth and her report back of her remarkable first day gleaning begin to renew her understanding of God. This comes out in the deliberate ambiguity of her statement: "May he be blessed of the Lord who has not withdrawn his kindness to the living and to the dead."[7] Is she talking here of Boaz, or of the Lord?

Meanwhile Boaz operates from a different perspective of God. If we see significance in the greetings between him and his reapers, there is a consciousness of the need for the Lord's presence and blessing.[8] He did not leave the inheritance, however difficult the times were. And yet he recognises that God's welcome and blessing is to all those who seek refuge under his "wings", even to a Moabitess. No bitterness or emptiness here as he prays for her wages to be "full from the Lord." In Chapter 3, he expresses once again his desire for the Lord's blessing, this time on Ruth.

The final and very significant mention of the Lord comes in 4:14 where it is the women who comment to Naomi about the significance of recent events: "Blessed is the Lord who has not left you without a redeemer today." This is at the climax of the book, immediately after the birth of Ruth's son. There is final recognition of the hand of God at work in human events, bringing Naomi back to himself and to his purposes through the provision of a redeemer.

CONCEPT OF SALVATION

This idea of the **redeemer** naturally brings us to another of our questions: what is the concept of salvation in the Book of Ruth? What is the gospel according to Ruth?

Ruth is a salvation story. It is the story of the return and restoration of Naomi not only to her inheritance but to her God. In addition, it is the story of how a Moabitess was converted to the one true God, and how, through her loyalty and faith, and the actions of a redeemer, God provided an heir, thus assuring the family line, the inheritance and the continuation of the royal line to David, and beyond to Messiah. Salvation is not just at the individual, personal level, but on the national level and, through the coming of Messiah, on the world level.

KEY IN THE FRONT DOOR

The Book of Ruth is a story, a literary work, divinely inspired. As a story it has a beginning, a middle and an end. We need to pay special attention to the way the book begins and ends, because it is often by placing these together that we will find keys to understanding the overall meaning. As we did with Philippians, we need to look for a **key in the front door**, but we also need to look for keys in the back door!

[6] Ruth 1:21

[7] Ruth 2:20

[8] Ruth 2:4

Consider how Ruth starts:

Now it came about in the days when the judges governed, that there was a famine in the land. And a certain man of Bethlehem in Judah went to sojourn in the land of Moab with his wife and his two sons. The name of the man was Elimelech, and the name of his wife, Naomi; and the names of his two sons were Mahlon and Chilion, Ephrathites of Bethlehem in Judah. Now they entered the land of Moab and remained there. Then Elimelech, Naomi's husband, died; and she was left with her two sons. They took for themselves Moabite women as wives; the name of the one was Orpah and the name of the other Ruth. And they lived there about ten years. Then both Mahlon and Chilion also died, and the woman was bereft of her two children and her husband.[9]

[9] Ruth 1:1-5

Now consider the ending:

So Boaz took Ruth, and she became his wife, and he went in to her. And the Lord enabled her to conceive, and she gave birth to a son. Then the women said to Naomi, "Blessed is the Lord who has not left you without a redeemer today, and may his name become famous in Israel. May he also be to you a restorer of life and a sustainer of your old age; for your daughter-in-law, who loves you and is better to you than seven sons, has given birth to him." Then Naomi took the child and laid him in her lap, and became his nurse. The neighbour women gave him a name, saying, "A son has been born to Naomi!" So they named him Obed. He is the father of Jesse, the father of David. Now these are the generations of Perez... and to Obed was born Jesse, and to Jesse, David.[10]

[10] Ruth 4:13-22

Take a few moments now to note down what strikes you as significant about both the beginning and the ending. In particular note **similarities** and **contrasts** between the two.

In terms of **similarities** we note the focus on Naomi, the listing of names, the emphasis on family and in particular on sons.

The **contrasts** are more numerous. From Moab, we are now in Israel. From the death of a husband and his sons, to the birth of a son; from famine, to the restoration and sustaining of life; from despair, to joy; from hopelessness, to a future; from the threatened end of the family name, to the establishment of the royal line that would lead to David.

The similarities and contrasts are not accidental. They are historically true. But the careful way in which the beginning and end of the book have been constructed is more than a hint that some of the major themes are to be found here. It is the author's way of guiding our interpretation of the story.

Let's note a number of other ways in which the author guides us. Notice, first, how he uses the women in Bethlehem to point up the true, spiritual significance of the events. This happens both later in Chapter 1 and at the end of Chapter 4. Secondly, note their final comment: "A son has been born to Naomi!" [11] This is quite a remarkable statement. The reality was that a son has been born to Ruth. But the women have not got it wrong. All along this has been **Naomi's story** – the story of the restoration of Naomi to God, to her inheritance, to hope through redemption of

[11] Ruth 4:17

the family and the birth of an heir. The women can see the true significance of Obed's birth.

The book also has a **middle.** This is where we find the main action and, as we have seen, it hinges on the Ruth-Boaz axis. The decision of Ruth to remain with Naomi and to believe in the God of Israel, together with the relationship between her and Boaz and his commitment to being the kinsman redeemer, are what takes us from the bleak winter of the opening verses to the new life and hope of spring at the end.

This is an outline sketch of the major thought-flow of the book. There is of course a great deal more than this as we consider each individual chapter, but we will have to leave that for your more detailed study!

It is time finally to try to put this all together and to establish first what the major lessons were for the original audience – I haven't forgotten that we are still talking about this! – and what the meaning and application might be for us today.

MAJOR THEMES AND LESSONS

A number of complementary ways of reading the Book of Ruth have emerged. The book is a very human story of return and restoration. It is also a profound account of the interactions of God within individual human history, and how basic decisions predicated on faith and loyalty towards God can impact not just a family but a nation. It is also the story of how the royal line was almost erased, and yet how it was remarkably restored, assuring the coming of the King. And since the prophets would announce that the world's Messiah was himself of the tribe of Judah and of the line of David, what was at stake in this story was the central purpose of God in human history – the fulfilment of the promises to Abraham through the coming of THE seed, the Messiah.

There are powerful lessons in each of these readings, first at the personal level: the disastrous consequences of turning their backs on their God-given inheritance thinking that far-off fields are greener; the wonderful providence of God as his hand works behind the scenes to bless his people; God's commitment to his purposes, and his power to achieve them; the incredible significance in God's purposes of seemingly simple, individual decisions in the area of family life, and of loyalty and love; a reminder of the need for redemption.

At the national level there were also deep lessons. In the times of the Judges Israel in general lost the sense of the reality of the presence and government of God. They still held it as a theological doctrine, no doubt, but doctrines on their own don't help. Like Elimelech – whose name, incidentally, means 'God is King' – they didn't remain loyal, especially when times got difficult. The result was chaos. It is surely not an accident that the story of Ruth is set in Bethlehem, not only the house of bread, but the city that witnesses the horrific lawlessness of gang rape and murder, which almost let to the total annihilation of an entire tribe. What was needed was a return to God, the rediscovery of faith and loyalty towards him. What happened at the micro level of a single family becomes a symbol of hope for a nation, pointing to where and how restoration could be found. In addition, under the providence of God, the faith-decisions of ordinary people led ultimately to national salvation under David. The book of Ruth moves from the chaos of the end of Judges to restoration of faith and hope, and the fulfilment of God's promise to provide a king.

APPLYING THE BOOK OF RUTH TODAY

First, we should apply the principle of **continuity** and ask which of the above lessons apply to us unchanged?

Many of them apply directly: the danger of allowing our decisions in life to be motivated by purely financial or human considerations; the importance of genuine conversion to God, and of loyalty to him; the providential activity of God in our lives; the practical examples of hard work, loyalty, friendship and love provided by this story; the move from bitterness and emptiness, to joy and fulfilment through the redemption God provides; our need of God's intervention and his provision of redemption.

Second, let's consider the principle of **discontinuity** and ask what contrasts are there between the specific Old Testament situation and our context under the New Covenant?

The issue of **inheritance** plays a critical role in the action of the Book of Ruth: Naomi's purpose was to "raise up the name of the dead upon his inheritance".[12] Why was this so important?

[12] Ruth 4:5

Under their great champion Joshua, the Promised Land was parcelled out, and each family in Israel was given their inheritance in the land (except for the Levites). This was done by means of casting lots, symbolising their desire to leave the choice up to God. As a result, they had the strong view that there was something sacred about each family's inheritance; it was not to be sold or squandered.[13]

[13] See the story in 1 Kings 21 of Naboth and his vineyard, and how he refused to sell it because he saw it as his God-given inheritance

This is what lies behind David's comments in Psalm 16: "The Lord is the portion of my inheritance and my cup; you support my lot. The lines have fallen to me in pleasant places; indeed, my heritage is beautiful to me." [14] The 'lines' are the boundary lines of a physical inheritance; but here David is referring to the Lord as his inheritance, and to all that he has in him. David has spiritualised the idea of inheritance, expanding it from what is given to the Giver himself. This in itself is something that we can apply to ourselves: it would make a remarkable difference to our attitude to our 'lot in life' if we were to adopt David's approach to life.

[14] Psalm 16:5,6

We are no longer in the same historical and theological context. I live in Northern Ireland. Despite rumours to the contrary, Northern Ireland is not the Promised Land! I own no territory in Northern Ireland, but I still have an inheritance in God himself, as David had. If I did own territory in Northern Ireland, it would still not be the Promised Land! It is not that God has no more interest in earthly real estate. The fact is that ultimately God owns everything – he is very interested in material things, and not just in spiritual, and his promise of real estate to Abraham and his seed appears to have been expanded to include the whole world, according to Paul in Romans 4:13. But for now we believers in Christ are not at the moment to think of our inheritance in terms of a particular land.

The New Testament expands the concept of inheritance still further, to a level that certainly was far beyond what Naomi had in mind. Peter tells us that we have been given "new birth into a living hope through the resurrection of Jesus Christ from the dead, and into an inheritance that can never perish, spoil or fade – kept in heaven..." [15]

[15] 1 Peter 1:3,4

In addition to this future inheritance towards which we travel, there is another sense in which the New Testament teaches we have already entered our inheritance. We are already seated with Christ in heavenly places.[16] All the treasures of wisdom

[16] Ephesians 2:6

[17]Colossians 2:2,3, 9,10

and knowledge are in Christ, and we are also in him.[17] This, therefore, is something that we can begin to enjoy now. We have incredible wealth in Christ. Once again, what a difference it would make if we saw life like this, rather than being consumed by the desire for wealth that will perish.

Sadly, some of us, like Elimelech, struggle to make a go of it. The grass is always greener on the other side of the fence. We know we should be cultivating our enjoyment of our inheritance in Christ, committing ourselves to God and to his Word of grace that is able to build us up and give us an inheritance.[18] But the financial realities of life, and life's bitter experiences often deflect our focus. What is needed is restoration to God, to the spiritual reality and wealth of our redemption and this love relationship into which we have been brought like Ruth, once outsiders and aliens but now brought near and incorporated into the family of God.

[18] Acts 20:32

And here it is almost impossible to resist the temptation to see in the Book of Ruth a prototype of a greater story. A prototype is a working model that give us some idea of what the advanced, full-developed version will be able to do. What might that greater story be?

It too is the story of a runaway world; of people who have been given an inheritance but who seek to enjoy it in defiance of the giver. And as a result they ruin the inheritance they have been given. How will it be put right? Through redemption and faith.

The central action of the Book of Ruth is of a Moabitess coming to faith in the one true God, and of Boaz, in his love, doing all that was needed to redeem Naomi, Ruth, together with the inheritance. Naomi sold out to Boaz, the kinsman redeemer, but in selling out, she received back far more than she gave.

When Jesus walked along the road toward Emmaus and explained to the two disciples the things concerning himself in all the Scriptures, I wonder did he mention the Book of Ruth? I wonder did he say, "To restore people to the father, to restore the inheritance, Messiah had to pay the price of redemption - don't you see it? Don't you remember Naomi's story, and Ruth and Boaz? It has been there all the time, and you didn't see it!"

CLOSE ENCOUNTERS

We have come to the end of this handbook but hopefully not to the end of our study of God's Word!

It sometimes happens that in the course of study of God's Word we actually lose sight of the goal of our study, and we become like people hugging a signpost at the roadside in the mistaken belief that they have arrived at their destination!

Some people in Jesus' day made the same mistake and he spoke to them about it: "You diligently study the Scriptures because you think that by them you possess eternal life. These are the Scriptures that testify about me, yet you refuse to come to me to have life." [1]

It is a sad error to confuse the end with the means, the destination with the signpost. They diligently studied - some could have recited the entire Old Testament. They wrote commentaries, analysed, discussed and argued. It was their life.

And yet it wasn't life for, as Jesus pointed out to them, they had missed the whole point: real life, eternal life, is about a person - the Person. The Scriptures everywhere pointed to him: they indicated what he would be like and what he would do, so that there wouldn't be the slightest difficulty in recognising him. But they mistook the signpost for the reality and they refused the close-up, personal encounter with Christ.

Our goal in studying Scripture is not to have a happier life, a better marriage, a more successful career. We are not looking for maxims to live by, 7 habits, 12 steps or 21 laws that will help us on. Our goal is not to learn how to control our tongue, how to cope with stress, how to be ourselves. Our goal is not even Bible knowledge on its own. **Our goal is to encounter Jesus Christ and through that encounter to be transformed.**

This is not to say, of course, that the words do not matter. There is a wonderful balance in the statements of Christ on this subject. As we read on from our present story into John 6, we find Jesus miraculously feeding a great crowd. For many in the crowd this was kingdom come. Why, with this man as their king, they would no

[1] John 5:39, 40

159

longer need the bakery, they would no longer need the health service - he could supply all their needs and desires. Here was the kind of leader they needed.

So they were going to make him king. Jesus withdrew, but they persisted. He crossed the lake, but they followed, albeit by a different method. Their following did not indicate a desire to know Christ, to commit to him as forgiver and director. It was simply to have their hunger satisfied once more. Just like the religious leaders before them, but in a different way, they had totally misunderstood. Jesus had not come to satisfy their physical needs and desires. Real life was higher and deeper than that.

So he began to spell out the implications of what it would mean to make him leader. He hadn't come to stay on their terms, in the world that they had refashioned in their own image and now wanted his help to maintain. He was on the move, to Jerusalem and the eternal beyond. Were they prepared to follow him, to see this world as only temporary and to get on board for an eternal journey? Were they prepared to share in his life and in his suffering? Or was it only a selfish pursuit - health, wealth and prosperity for the asking?

First they began to grumble, and then they began to argue. Then they gave up on the whole idea, turned on their heels and walked away. Jesus turned to his small group: "You do not want to leave too, do you?" Peter replied: "Lord, to whom shall we go? You have the words of eternal life." [2]

Words of eternal life. The words are important, vitally important. As Jesus said to them on the same occasion "The words I have spoken to you are spirit and they are life."[3] The problem many of the would-be but now would-not-be followers, as Jesus himself pointed out, was that fundamentally they were not believers.

And here is the **balance.** We must not make the mistake of thinking that through studying the Bible we have eternal life and that the more we study, the more life we earn. At the same time we must not make the mistake of saying, "I don't need the words. I've got Jesus!" Jesus has given us his words. **To take him seriously, is to take his words seriously.** (I can't imagine my wife responding positively to being told, "I love you - but I've no interest in anything you say.")

In a study guide like this, it is perhaps easy for some of us to make the mistake of thinking that the study of God's Word is all work and no reward, all human effort, no divine presence. But the Bible is a God-breathed, living Book. If we allow him, God will take us to deeper and deeper levels of spiritual reality through it. The Word is living and active. It is constantly doing its work. The Spirit dwells within us desiring nothing better than to bring honour and prominence to Jesus Christ through revealing him to us.

Encountering God is not some remote goal, but a present reality. The same chapter of John contains the following fascinating event. Immediately after the miraculous feeding of the five thousand men, the disciples set off across the lake for Capernaum. Darkness falls and the winds rise, and still Jesus has not joined them. Suddenly, just over three miles out, they see Jesus walking to join them. Terror grips them. This is not a normal circumstance. But they invite Jesus into their boat, convinced that it is really he.

And then comes the twist in the tail. Immediately Jesus gets into the boat **they find themselves at their destination.** [4] Don't ask me how it was done physically and geographically. I don't know (yet). But I've begun to understand how it is spiritually that you can be **travelling** to a destination and at the same time **be there**, because Jesus is there.

[2] John 6:68

[3] John 6:63

[4] John 6:21

160

Does this make sense? We are on a journey - an amazing goal awaits us. But it is not 'pie in the sky when we die'. Jesus travels with us. And because he is with us, there is a sense in which we are already at our destination. We don't receive eternal life when we die or when Christ returns. We have it already, if we have put our trust in Christ. We don't simply get to meet Jesus when we die or when he returns. We meet him now, at a very deep and intimate level, through his Word, by his Spirit.

So look for him, and respond to him. You will need hard work. You will also need prayer. You will need all the brain power you possess. You will also need the Spirit. God will speak through his Word into your life.

There are times when Paul is writing that he is so overwhelmed by the revelation he has been given that he can't help but respond in worship to God. For example, Romans 9, 10 and 11 contain some of the most profound concepts in the whole of the Bible. Yet Paul's response is to say:

> *Oh, the depth of the riches of the wisdom and knowledge of God! How unsearchable his judgements, and his paths beyond tracing out! Who has known the mind of the Lord? Or who has been his counsellor? Who has ever given to God, that God should repay him? For from him and through him and to him are all things. To him be the glory for ever! Amen.* [5]

[5] Romans 11:33-36

You have started – now you must continue. The Bible is a large world; the more we explore it, the bigger it will become. And at each stage of life we will discover that God has truth for us that will liberate our thinking, feed our souls and equip us for an examined, full life.

POST SCRIPT

I would love to know how you are getting on, and to hear both your thoughts about what was especially helpful or unhelpful in this guide and suggestions for what could/should be included next time around.

Please feel free to contact me on email: gilbert.lennox@glenabbey.org.uk

SELECT BIBLIOGRAPHY

There are a number of risks in providing a list of suggested books. First, that I give the impression that I have read them all! This is not the case. Most of the texts I will list are reference books, not designed to be read at a sitting. Second, that I endorse everything that is said in every book. (Not having read every word, I could hardly do that.) The third danger is that you are overwhelmed and discouraged by even the mention of these titles. Please don't be. None is absolutely necessary to your enjoyment of God's Word. Yet even one or two of them could provide you with enormous benefit and this may well generate a taste for more. Fourth, that you bankrupt yourself in attempting to purchase them all at once. It takes time to build a library. I encourage you to take the time, select carefully, and over the years fill a bookshelf at least with books such as these which are designed to help you to get the message.

BOOKS ON HERMENEUTICS (the science and art of biblical interpretation)

Grasping God's Word, by J Scott Duvall and J Daniel Hays, Zondervan, 2001
In its own words this is designed to be a 'hands-on approach to reading, interpreting and applying the Bible.' It is aimed at university students (undergraduate level) and arose out of a concern on the part of the authors that at evangelical Christian colleges in America many students are not being taught how to read the biblical story for themselves.
It differs from Getting the Message particularly in that it does not dwell long on any one individual book of the Bible. At the same time, it expands on many of the issues raised in this guide – it has 431 pages! - and introduces more beside. So if you are looking for something to help you build on the skills you have been learning here I have not come across a better book than this. In addition, for those wishing to build

a personal library, and I hope you are, their Appendix 2 has hundreds of suggestions for reference books and commentaries, plus their own recommended short-list. **Strongly recommended.**

How to read the Bible for all its worth, Gordon Fee and Douglas Stuart, Scripture Union, 2nd Ed, 1994
The chief focus of this excellent book is on the different literary genres that make up the Bible and on how to read each to maximum profit. There is a very healthy and practical focus throughout on hermeneutical issues, and in particular on understanding what Scripture meant for its original audience and how we should translate that meaning into our modern contexts. **Strongly recommended.**

The Art of Biblical Narrative, Robert Alter, Basic Books, 1981 (ISBN 0-465-00427-X)
This book won the National Jewish Book Award for Jewish Thought. We may not agree with all of Alter's conclusions – for example, he believes that "Ruth, Naomi and Boaz are fictional inventions, probably based on no more than names, if that, preserved in national memory" - but as a guide to how to read the Old Testament as literature I think it would be hard to find better. I include the ISBN number as it may be more difficult to obtain than most of the others in my list. **Strongly recommended.**

New Testament Exegesis, Gordon D Fee, Westminster John Knox Press, 3rd Ed, 2002
This work is also aimed at students (undergraduate and above) and could be quite tough going, although worth persevering with for there is much to learn here. It focuses quite quickly on the small picture of textual analysis – perhaps too quickly? There are some specific sections for those working with the original Greek, although this is not necessary for following the core principles. Indeed Fee suggests from his own experience that those who do not know Greek but who follow the exegetical principles carefully do as well in their exegesis as those who know the language. One chapter is aimed at those who preach and teach – for them the book might well be worth it for this chapter alone.

Living by the Book, Howard C Hendricks and William D Hendricks, Moody, 1991
Written at a more accessible and popular level, this book is engagingly written and has many practical exercises and useful insights.

Is there a message in this text? Kevin J. Vanhoozer, Apollos, 1998
A fascinating book, helpful in particular for those grappling with post-modern theories of hermeneutics, but not for the faint hearted!

BOOKS ON BIBLE BACKGROUND

The IVP Bible Background Commentary: New Testament, Craig S Keener, IVP, 1993
This resource follows the text of each New Testament book, providing a wealth of

cultural and historical information as and when it is relevant to an understanding of particular statements. **Strongly recommended.**

The IVP Bible Background Commentary: Old Testament, John. H Walton, Mark W Chavalas, Victor H Matthews, IVP, 2000
This does the same for the Old Testament. **Strongly recommended.**

Encountering the New Testament, Walter A Elwell and Robert W Yarborough, Baker, 1998
Colourful and informative, written at a popular level and very attractively presented. It includes a CD. **Strongly recommended.**

An Introduction to the New Testament, D A Carson, Douglas J Moo and Leon Morris, Apollos, 1992
The primary focus of this work is on historical questions dealing with authorship, date, sources, purpose, destination and so on for each New Testament book, but it also includes a brief outline of contents. Chapter 7 is a very informative introduction to Paul, and a 12-page section is devoted to Philippians.

An Introduction to the Old Testament, Raymond B. Dillard, Tremper Longman III, Zondervan, 1994
Does for the Old Testament what the above does for the New.

BIBLE DICTIONARIES

The New Bible Dictionary, Eds I Howard Marshall, A R Millard, J I Packer, D J Wiseman, IVP, 1996 has vast amounts of helpful information on all kinds of Bible topics. **Strongly recommended.**

The Illustrated Bible Dictionary, Ed J D Douglas, 3 Vols., IVP, 1980 is based on the text of the 1962 New Bible Dictionary, although revised with many new articles, and, as its name suggests, has many very helpful photographs, maps and other illustrations, both in colour and in black and white.

The Dictionary of Biblical Imagery, Ed Leland Ryken, James C Wilhoit, Tremper Longman III, IVP, 1998 – is an "encyclopaedic exploration of the images, symbols, motifs, metaphors, figures of speech and literary patterns of the Bible." Utterly fascinating. **Strongly recommended.**

CONCORDANCES

Zondervan NIV Exhaustive Concordance, Edward W Goodrick, John R Kohlenberger, 2nd Edition, Zondervan, 1999
Not for carrying around in your pocket! But certainly exhaustive. There is an equivalent Zondervan concordance for the NASB. **Strongly recommended.**

The Greek-English Concordance to the New Testament, John R Kohlenberger, Edward Goodrick, James A Swanson, Zondervan, 1997
Lists all occurrences of each Greek word in the New Testament, and therefore particularly helpful for word studies.

WORD STUDIES

Vine's Complete Expository Dictionary of Old and New Testament Words, Eds W E Vine, Merrill F Unger, William White Jr, Thomas Nelson, 1980
Helpful and easy to follow.

The NIV Theological Dictionary of New Testament Words, Ed Verlyn Verbrugge, Zondervan, 2000
Does exactly what it says on the cover.

COMMENTARIES

The variety of available commentaries in English can be overwhelming, with new volumes appearing every year. Most of us could not afford to keep up! This is where having access to a good theological library or study centre is an immense boon. I suggest that you build your own library slowly, buying a commentary or two (if possible) on the biblical text you are currently studying.

There are a number of one volume commentaries for the whole Bible and that would be an excellent place to start. Arguable the best of these is:

New Bible Commentary, Eds G J Wenham, J A Motyer, D A Carson, R T France, IVP, 1994

In terms of individual commentaries, I have experience of using volumes from the following three series in particular:

The Bible Speaks Today series, published by IVP
This is one of the best series of commentaries for the general reader, with such well -known writers as John Stott and Alec Motyer, who writes the volume on Philippians.

The NIV Life Application Commentary series, published by Zondervan
This series is probably a step up in quantity of information and yet equally readable. The commentary on Philippians is written by Frank Thielman. The commentary on Ruth is written by K Lawson Younger Jr.

The New International Commentary series on Old and New Testaments, published by Eerdmans
The commentaries in this series are more detailed and scholarly, and I've found them particularly helpful for reference. The commentary on Philippians is written by Gordon Fee.